NIRU GUPTA'S
EVERYDAY INDIAN

MEREHURST

CONTENTS

To all loved ones whose brains and talents I picked, and special thanks to my husband, Mahendra, daughter, Kirti, and son-in-law, Rakesh, for their support and, of course, their courage and patience in being tasters and critics of my numerous trials.

Published in 1995 by Merehurst Limited
Ferry House, 51-57 Lacy Road, Putney, London SW15 1PR

ISBN 1-85391-430-4

Editor: Beverly Le Blanc
Series designer: Roger Hammond
Designers: Roger Daniels and Mike Rose
Photographer: Ken Field
Home economist: Kerenza Harries
Home economist's assistant: Jo Craig
Stylist: Suzy Gittins
Typesetter: Nigel Burns

Colour separation by Global Colour, Malaysia
Printed in Singapore by CS Graphics Pte Ltd

N O T E

A standard spoon measurement is used in all recipes:

1 teaspoon = one 5 ml spoon
All spoon measures are level

Ovens should be preheated to the specified temperature.

For all recipes, quantities are given metric and imperial. Follow one set of measures but not a mixture as they are not interchangeable.

INTRODUCTION

How to cook an everyday Indian meal is what this book is all about. These are the recipes I, my friends and our cooks prepare daily.

Many Indian families have a cook, so it isn't unusual to find cooking not taken seriously in Indian homes. When we each reached the age of sixteen, myself and my four sisters were goaded into the kitchen, but without much success, as was the case with all the daughters in most of the families we knew. Little did I know how much of a passion cooking would become for me. A lot of the credit for this development goes to my husband, who is not only fond of eating but also very critical of what he eats. The latter feature was quite annoying at times, but has stood me in good stead in the long run. To top it all, as my daughter grew up she turned out to be an even greater critic. I often tell her she should take up a taster's job!

After I was married, I gradually found myself cooking and reading about cooking more and more. In fact, I can remember visiting an aunt and having her observe 'Oh my, this one even takes cookery books for bedtime reading!'

I grew up as a vegetarian, but my initiation into cooking food with meat came under the guidance of my husband, when he had just returned from being a student in the United States. There he had become familiar with cooking, but otherwise, it is very rare to meet an Indian male who cooks at home. Therefore, when anyone says that cooking is difficult, I tell them it is merely a matter of interest and perseverance.

One piece of advice I always give to my students is that to be fair to any author you should follow a recipe accurately the first time to get the desired result, and then you can make your own additions and subtractions. I also advise you to use authentic ingredients, even if it means making the effort to go to an Indian grocer. Once you get the Indian ingredients, you will capture that delicious Indian flavour that makes a dish authentic.

Indian cooking, like any other, is such that once you know the basic methods, you can invent your own recipes. I have arranged most of this book in menu form so you won't have difficulty planning, but at the same time there are enough recipes to allow you the liberty to change menus according to your taste. I explain how simple it is to make up large quantities of masalas in advance, so they are ready to cook with a variety of more familiar everyday ingredients. When time is short, you will find that using a ready made masala is just as quick as opening a jar of curry from the supermarket, and so much better tasting!

I sincerely hope you will enjoy using this book and it introduces you to some new Indian dishes.

MASALAS

Top to bottom: Green Masala, see page 11;
Red Masala, see page 10; Garam Masala, see page 9

In Indian cookery there are some basic masalas: combinations of spices, that are used for different recipes. You can mix and match the spices and their uses according to your taste, and you will soon realise how handy they are to quickly add extra flavour and spice to meals. It is the combination of ingredients put into masalas that makes the same dish taste different in different homes. Most of the masalas in this book are available at supermarkets, but I always like to make my own. It is when these spices are freshly ground, as my sister Gita does in her little coffee grinder, that dishes taste best. Still you can make masalas in larger quantities so you always have them on hand.

Masalas can be either a combination of ground spices or cooked mixtures. I advise you to store the dry masalas in airtight containers so they stay fresh and are ready to use whenever you want them. These are best made with the weather is dry, so there is less chance of bacteria forming. The shelf life, if tightly sealed, will be several months.

You can also make the cooked masalas in large enough quantities that you can use them for several meals because they will keep for 15 to 20 days in the refrigerator.

GARAM MASALA

Time to make: 10 to 15 minutes
Makes about 315 g (10 oz)

60 g (2 oz) black cardamom pods
155 g (5 oz) cumin seeds
30 g (1 oz) cinnamon stick
30 g (1 oz) cloves
30 g (1 oz) black peppercorns
4 bay leaves

Cook's Tip
The cardamom shells are good for flavouring liquids, so don't throw them away.

Used to flavour all kinds of savoury dishes, garam masala is often simply called curry powder. Although you can easily buy garam masala, I hope you will make your own, varying my recipe to suit your family's tastes. Feel free to add a bit more of one spice or a bit less of another. It is important to make sure all the ingredients are perfectly dry before you begin grinding them together, otherwise they will tend to bunch up together and not grind.

1 Crush the black cardamom pods using your fingertips, then remove the shells and extract the tiny seeds.
2 Put the cardamom seeds, cumin seeds, cinnamon stick, cloves, peppercorns and bay leaves in a blender or food processor and process until a fine powder forms. Store in an airtight container.

SPICY MASALA

Chaat Ka Masala

Time to make: 20 minutes
Makes about 1 kg (2 lb)

155 g (5 oz) coriander seeds
220 g (7 oz) cumin seeds
60 g (2 oz) ajwain seeds
315 g (10 oz) rock salt
155 g (5 oz) ground dried mango
60 g (2 oz) dried mint
45 g (1½ oz) citric acid
2 tablespoons garam masala
2 tablespoons peppercorns

Chaat means anything that is spicy, tangy and snacky, and this is a versatile masala ideal for garnishing spicy and tangy dishes. It is also equally good as a garnish for vegetables to be eaten raw as a salad and on boiled potatoes or sweet potatoes. Even in India, most cooks buy this ready-made, but this is the recipe from my aunt, Pushpa Masiji, who always makes her own.

1 Roast the coriander seeds in a heavy-based frying pan or wok over a high heat, stirring constantly, until dark brown. Pour out of the pan and set aside to cool for about 5 minutes.
2 Roast the cumin and ajwain seeds in the same pan. Pour the seeds out of the pan and set aside.
3 Put all the seeds, rock salt, ground mango, mint, citric acid, garam masala and peppercorns in a blender or food processor and process until a fine powder forms. Store in an airtight container.

RED MASALA
Reshad

Time to make: 10 minutes
Time to cook: 10 minutes
Makes enough to cook with 1 kg
    (2 lb) vegetables or meat

500 g (1 lb) onions
250 g (8 oz) tomatoes
22 g (¾ oz) tamarind pulp, diluted with 4 tablespoons water
1 tablespoon each chopped garlic, salt and sugar
4 cloves
3 or 4 whole dried red chillies
large pinch ground cinnamon
60 ml (2 fl oz) vegetable oil

I was taught this masala by Sailor, my parent's Goan cook. It gets its name from the dried red chillies that colour it, so only buy the brightest dried red chillies.

1   Roughly chop half the onions and thinly slice the remainder. Finely chop the tomatoes and set aside.
2   Put the chopped onions, diluted tamarind, garlic, salt, sugar, cloves, red chillies and ground cinnamon in a blender or food processor and process until a paste forms.
3   Heat the oil in a heavy-based saucepan over a medium heat. Add the sliced onions and stir-fry until they brown. Stir in the chopped tomatoes and continue stir-frying until the fat separates.
4   Stir in the onion paste and continue stir-frying until the fat separates again. Remove from the heat and leave to cool, then cover and refrigerate for up to 20 days.

TOMATO MASALA
Tamattar Pyaaz Ka Masala

Time to make: 10 minutes
Time to cook: 10 minutes
Makes enough to cook with
    500 g (1 lb) vegetables or meat

250 g (8 oz) onions
125 g (4 oz) tomatoes
1 teaspoon chopped garlic
1 teaspoon chopped ginger
60 ml (2 fl oz) vegetable oil
1 teaspoon cumin seeds
2 bay leaves
1 tablespoon ground coriander
1 tablespoon salt
½ teaspoon each turmeric, garam masala and chilli powder

A rich, thick masala with tomatoes and onions for cooking vegetables and meat.

1   Roughly chop the onions and grate the tomatoes; set the tomatoes aside.
2   Put the onions, garlic and ginger in a blender or food processor and process until a paste forms.
3   Heat the oil in a heavy-based saucepan or wok over a medium heat and add the cumin seeds and bay leaves. When the seeds splutter, stir in the onion paste and stir-fry until it becomes brown and the fat separates.
4   Stir in the tomatoes, coriander, salt, turmeric, garam masala and chilli powder and continue stir-frying until the fat separates again. Remove from the heat and leave to cool, then cover and refrigerate for up to 20 days.

GREEN MASALA
Hara Masala

Time to make: 10 minutes
Makes enough to marinate 1 kg
  (2 lb) chicken, fish, meat,
  paneer or vegetables

45 g (1½ oz) coriander leaves
2 or 3 fresh green chillies
1 tablespoon salt
2 teaspoons chopped ginger
2 teaspoons chopped garlic
1 teaspoon roughly chopped cinnamon stick
seeds from 2 black cardamoms
8 black peppercorns
8 cloves
60 ml (2 fl oz) lemon juice

A speciality of the western regions of India around Goa. I use this uncooked masala to marinate chicken, fish, meat, paneer or vegetables, rubbing it into the chosen ingredients. Leave for several hours, or overnight, then grill or cook over a low heat with a little water. I thank my friend Lalita for this recipe.

1 Roughly chop the coriander leaves and the chillies.
2 Put the coriander leaves, salt, ginger, garlic, cinnamon, green chillies, cardamom seeds, peppercorns and cloves in a blender or food processor and process until well combined.
3 Add the lemon juice and process again until the mixture is well combined. This will keep in a covered container in the fridge for up to 2 weeks.

DRY TANDOORI MASALA

Time to make: 10 minutes
Makes about 330 g (11 oz)

155 g (5 oz) salt
30 g (1 oz) each dried ginger, garlic powder and dried ground onion
20 g (¾ oz) chilli powder
15 g (½ oz) ground pepper
2 tablespoons chaat ka masala
2 tablespoons garam masala
4 tablespoons fenugreek leaves

Unlike the masala used in the Tandoori Chicken recipe, see page 38, this mixture of ground spices will keep almost indefinitely in an airtight container. To use this, simply mix 3 tablespoons of it with 3 tablespoons malt vinegar or 250 g (8 oz) plain yogurt, which will yield enough to cook 1 kg (2 lb) meat, fish or chicken with bones or 500 g (1 lb) without bones. Add 1 teaspoon powdered red food colouring, if you want.

Mix all the ingredients together. Store in an airtight container.

PICKLES AND RELISH

Top to bottom: Onion Relish with Mint, see page 37;
Ginger and Lemon Relish, see page 17; Lime Pickle, see page 16

Pickles are very important in Indian cooking. In fact, it would be difficult to count the number of pickles produced in India. An entire book just on the subject of Indian pickles is quite justified, as each region has its own speciality pickles. The mango and lemon ones are popular throughout the whole country, but they taste quite different everywhere because of the different spices used.

Traditionally, pickles were made in large quantities to last the whole year. These days, however, there are few of us who still make the effort to make pickles at home, since such a large variety is available in the markets, and time and space are at such a premium. But, offer a home-made pickle to anyone and you will see how much they enjoy it!

Chutneys are a general accompaniment to meals in India, and they fall halfway between masalas and pickles in their preparation and use. These are found on the table, the difference being that these are usually made from fresh ingredients, although some can be cooked. (I haven't included any cooked chutneys in this book.) The most popular are coriander and mint chutneys. Some chutneys are also cooked with other ingredients, such as a masala mixture.

MANGO PICKLE

Aam Ka Achar

Time to make: 45 minutes, plus
  7 to 10 days maturing
Makes about 4.5 kg (9 lb)

2.5 kg (5 lb) mangoes
250 g (8 oz) salt
100 g (3½ oz) fenugreek seeds
100 g (3½ oz) fennel seeds
45 g (1½ oz) chilli powder
45 g (1½ oz) onion seeds
45 g (1½ oz) turmeric
45 g (1½ oz) whole dried red chillies
30 g (1 oz) black peppercorns
about 1.5 litres (48 fl oz) mustard oil

Cook's Tip
In London, instead of using mangoes, I find this is an excellent way to make the most of hard, tart apples, which are impossible to eat unsweetened.

This is my grandmother's recipe, and is typical of the pickles made in northern India. The large quantity is because when she made this pickle, she intended for it to last a whole year. I carry on her tradition and make my batch each summer.

The most important thing to remember is to make sure the pickle is always covered with a layer of oil. The oil forms an airtight seal and acts as a preservative. If you don't have room for a large container, put this into several sterilised storage jars and keep them in a cool, dark place until required.

My grandmother would have sterilised the storage jar by leaving it in the hot sun, but I suggest you buy sterilising liquid or tablets from a chemist's. After washing the container, give it a rinse in the solution and then let it dry. My sister in London keeps her jars of pickles by the radiator when the sun isn't strong enough to mature the mixture. My family particularly likes this pickle with parathas, pooris and naans.

1 Rinse the mangoes well, then stone them and cut them into the desired sizes. Do not peel them.
2 Put the salt, fenugreek seeds, fennel seeds, chilli powder, onion seeds, turmeric, dried red chillies and peppercorns in a large bowl and mix together well. Stir in about 250 ml (8 fl oz) of the oil, stirring until well blended and the mixture becomes slightly damp.
3 Sprinkle a layer of spice mixture into the sterilised storage jar. Add a couple of handfuls of the mango pieces to the remaining spice mixture and mix well by hand, rubbing the spice mixture and mangoes together until all the mango pieces are coated. Put the mangoes into the jar and repeat until all the mangoes are in the jar. Top up with any spice mixture that remains. This ensures that the mangoes do not spoil.
4 Cover the jar tightly with a lid, then place the jar outside in the sun for 2 to 3 days, shaking it 2 or 3 times a day.
5 On the fourth day, add the remaining oil, adding extra if necessary to cover the contents. Put the jar in the sun for another 3 to 4 days and leave it without shaking it again. It will then be ready to eat but becomes more tender in a month's time.

STUFFED RED PEPPER PICKLE

Sabut Lal Mirch Ka Achar

Time to make: about 10 minutes,
  plus cooling
Time to cook: about 5 minutes
Makes about 500 g (1 lb)

---

500 g (1 lb) red peppers (see introduction)

90 g (3 oz) salt

75 g (2½ oz) ground dried mango

60 g (2 oz) ground coriander

60 g (2 oz) ground fennel seeds

185 ml (6 fl oz) mustard oil

The first time I had these was about 15 years ago when a relative brought them from Varnnasiin in northern India, and I liked them so much I immediately set out to learn how to make them. It was trial and error for some time but I eventually developed this recipe. The key to success is to use the correct type of pepper: look for long red peppers, rather than the plump, bell-shaped ones. They are mild, rather than spicy hot. I particularly enjoy these with plain bread, such as a Naan, see page 47.

1 Slit the peppers lengthways on one side from the base of the stalk to the tip, to create an opening for the filling. Snip it a little on one side at the broad end to make it easier to fill. Remove the seeds if you do not want these to be too hot.
2 Put the salt, ground dried mango, ground coriander and fennel seeds in a bowl and mix together. Stir in 60 ml (2 fl oz) of the oil.
3 Stuff the peppers with the spice mixture, pressing it in firmly.
4 Heat the remaining oil a heavy-based saucepan or a wok over a high heat. When you notice some movement in the oil and its fragrance becomes very strong, add the stuffed peppers. Cook, stirring occasionally with a long-handled spoon, for about 5 minutes until the peppers begin to look glossy and slightly cooked. Turn off the heat and leave the peppers and oil to cool.
5 When the peppers and oil are completely cool, transfer them to a sterilised, airtight jar, then screw on the lid. The peppers are then ready to eat but they will be tenderer and the flavour will mature if you leave them for a few days.

MIXED VEGETABLE PICKLE

Gobhi Shalgam Ka Acha

Time to make: 20 minutes
Time to cook: 25 to 30 minutes
Makes about 5 kg (10 lb)

1.5 kg (3 lb) carrots
1 kg (2 lb) turnips
1.5 kg (3 lb) cauliflower
125 g (4 oz) fresh root ginger
125 g (4 oz) cloves garlic
500 ml (16 fl oz) mustard oil
375 ml (12 fl oz) malt vinegar
250 g (8 oz) molassas
125 g (4 oz) mustard seeds, ground to a powder
125 g (4 oz) garam masala, see page 9
60 g (2 oz) chilli powder
125 g (4 oz) salt

Cook's Tip
This highly spiced pickle absorbs a lot of oil, so check the jar every couple of weeks and top up with extra heated oil, if necessary.

A spicy pickle recipe from northern India, this is made in a large quantity so it lasts a whole year, and the recipe was given to me my mother who, in turn, was given it by her mother. I invite my sisters over on the day I make this, and we have it for lunch with just white bread fresh from the bakery.

1 Cut the carrots and turnips into the desired sized pieces, matching each other and remembering that the cauliflower cooks faster than both of them. Break the cauliflower into florets. Rinse all the vegetables well, then spread them out to dry.
2 Peel and finely chop the ginger. Put the garlic and ginger in a mortar and use a pestle to pound together until they form a coarse paste. Alternatively, use the side of a wide-bladed knife to pound them together.
3 Put all the oil in a heavy-based pan or wok that is large enough to hold all the vegetables, with enough room to stir-fry. Heat the oil over a high heat until when a piece of vegetable is thrown in it bubbles up at once. Add the garlic and ginger paste and stir-fry for 5 to 6 minutes until it turns light brown.
4 Meanwhile, put the vinegar in a heavy-based saucepan over another burner and heat. Stir in the molassas and bring to the boil, then simmer, uncovered, until it dissolves.
5 When the garlic and ginger paste is light brown, stir in the carrots, turnips and cauliflower florets and continue stirring for about 15 minutes until the liquid given off by the vegetables when they were added to the hot oil has evaporated. The vegetable liquid will turn the oil hazy at first but when the liquid evaporates the oil will be clear again.
6 Still over a high heat, stir in the ground mustard seeds, garam masala, chilli powder and salt, then stir in the vinegar solution. Bring to the boil, then remove the pan or wok from the heat and leave the vegetables to cool.
7 When cool enough to handle, transfer the vegetables and pickling mixture to a sterilised, airtight jar, then store in a cool, dark place for up to one year.

LIME PICKLE
Nimbu Ka Achar

Time to make: about 10 minutes,
    plus 1 week to mature
Makes about 1.5 kg (3 lb)

---

1 kg (2 lb) limes

250 ml (8 fl oz) sesame oil

For the masala

45 g (1½ oz) cumin seeds

60 g (2 oz) sugar

2 tablespoons ground ginger

2 tablespoons ground lovage

**1 tablespoon each ground
cardamom, ground cloves,
ground cinnamon and ground
black pepper**

2 or 3 dried bay leaves, ground

60 g (2 oz) rock salt, ground

180 g (6 oz) salt

Don't expect this to be like the lime pickle you find in most Indian restaurants. It isn't made with hot spices, but instead with ones known for their digestive qualities. In some homes, jars of this are kept for years but mine never lasts that long.

1   Roast the cumin seeds in a heavy-based frying pan or wok over a medium heat, stirring constantly, until dark brown. Immediately pour the seeds out of the pan and set aside to cool, then grind them into a fine powder.
2   Combine the ground cumin seeds with the remaining masala ingredients and set aside.
3   Rinse the limes well, pat dry with kitchen towels, then cut into the desired sizes. Put them in a bowl with the masala mixture and mix together well.
4   Heat the sesame oil in a large heavy-based frying pan or wok over a high heat. Add the limes and masala mixture and stir-fry for about 5 minutes until the limes start to look glossy and are well coated with the mixture.
5   Spoon into a sterilised jar, then leave to cool. Screw on the lid and store in a cool, dry place for at least 1 week.

GINGER AND LEMON RELISH
Adrak Ka Kass

Time to make: 10 minutes
Makes about 220 g (7 oz)

---

220 g (7 oz) fresh root ginger

**1 tablespoon finely chopped
fresh green chillies, optional**

2 teaspoons lemon juice

1 teaspoon salt

Made with fresh ginger, I serve this relish with meals throughout the year, and it is especially popular with my in-laws. I am fortunate in that the fresh ginger in India is soft and tender with hardly any skin. But I have also made this with ginger bought in London and the results are quite good. Ginger aids digestion, so this is an ideal relish to enhance a heavy meal.

1   Peel the ginger. Slice thinly widthways, then slice as thinly as possible into shreds.

2 Put the ginger, chillies, if desired, lemon juice and salt in a bowl and stir together.

3 Cover tightly and refrigerate for 2 to 3 days, although I think this is best fresh.

PICKLED GREEN CHILLIES

Hari Mirch Ka Achar

Time to make: 5 minutes, plus cooling
Time to cook: about 10 minutes
Makes about 250 g (8 oz)

250 g (8 oz) fresh long, green chillies

125 ml (4 fl oz) malt vinegar

125 g (4 oz) brown sugar or molasses

60 ml (2 fl oz) groundnut or sesame oil

4 tablespoons ground cumin

4 tablespoons ground coriander

4 tablespoons salt

When I make these, I like the hot, fiery taste imparted by the chilli seeds, but you can make a milder version by removing the seeds. Just slit each chilli lengthways, then use the tip of a knife to remove the seeds and then chop.

1 Cut each green chilli into 2 or 3 pieces.

2 Put the vinegar and brown sugar or molasses in a heavy-based saucepan over a medium heat and stir until well mixed together. Cook, stirring, until the sugar melts and a syrup forms.

3 Heat the oil in another heavy-based saucepan or wok over a high heat. When you notice some movement on the surface of the oil and its fragrance becomes stronger, add the chillies. Cook, stirring constantly with a long handled spoon, for about 3 minutes until the chillies begin to look glossy.

4 Add the ground cumin, ground coriander and salt, stirring until the chillies are well coated with spices. Stir in the syrup and bring to the boil.

5 Turn off the heat and leave the chillies and oil to cool. When the chillies and oil are completely cool, transfer them to a sterilised, airtight jar, then screw on the lid and store in a cool, dark place. The chillies are ready to eat and do not benefit from being left to mature more than several days.

BASIC TECHNIQUES

MAKING GHEE

Many Indians favour ghee rather than vegetable oils or butter for cooking because of its rich, nutty flavour. In fact, I can remember when vegetable oils were rarely used in everyday cooking except for making pickles and for deep-frying. But then ghee became notorious for its high cholesterol level and vegetable oil was promoted as the healthier choice. It is purely for this reason that I do not use ghee in most of my recipes, but you can easily substitute it if you want for health reasons, I usually use sunflower or groundnut oil when I cook.

Ghee is similar to clarified butter and does not burn when used at high temperatures because the milk solids and moisture have been separated from the butter fat. You will find ghee sold in cans and packets at Indian grocers and large supermarkets, or you can make your own.

To make about 400 g (14 oz) ghee, melt 500 g (1 lb) butter in a heavy-based saucepan over a low heat. When the butter has melted, increase the heat until the butter foams, then stir once and lower the heat again. Leave to simmer, uncovered, for 15 to 20 minutes until the milk solids settle to the bottom and are a golden colour and the liquid on top is transparent. The exact time will depend on the butter's water content.

Meanwhile, line a sieve with muslin and place it over a bowl. Strain the transparent liquid though the muslin, taking great care not to pour in any sediment. The strained liquid is ghee, which will solidify once it has cooled. It can then be stored at room temperature, at about 25C, 76F, in a sealed container for a year. The sediment can be discarded, but in some Indian homes it is sautéed with semolina or flour and used to make sweet or savoury dishes.

MAKING PASTES

To make a paste from a large quantity of ingredients, I suggest you use a blender or food processor, but when you are using smaller quantities, I think it is just as easy to use a pestle and mortar.

You will see that many of the recipes in this book begin by pounding several ingredients together to make a fine or coarse paste. There is certainly no hard and fast rule about which texture you use, except to follow the recipe.

The differences are more a reflection of regional cooking than anything else. In some regions, for example, very little onion is used in the pastes, whereas in the South it is almost always used. But now there is much inter-mingling, and lots of methods have been mixed up or adopted from one region to another, especially for exotic cooking. How coarse or fine you make a paste certainly affects the texture of the overall dish. In some dishes, I like to bite into the onions or tomatoes, whereas I like others to be smooth.

COOKING AND TEMPERING LENTILS

There is no end to the variety of lentils and the ways they are prepared in India, and tempering is a very simple technique for adding extra flavour to cooked lentils. In India, every family has its own 'recipe'.

The exact amount of water you use for cooking lentils is very much a matter of if you prefer a thick or thin consistency. As a general rule, however, I suggest you start with three times the volume of split lentils or four times the volume for whole lentils.

Cook 185 g (6 oz) lentils over a high heat until the water comes to the boil, then lower the heat and simmer, partly covered, until they reach the desired consistency. If you want to add yogurt, dried mango or tamarind, this is when to do it, then you can temper the lentils.

To flavour 185 g (6 oz) cooked lentils, stir 1 teaspoon cumin seeds and a large pinch of ground asafoetida in 2 tablespoons hot melted ghee, then stir together with the lentils.

Or melt 2 tablespoons ghee or heat 2 tablespoons vegetable oil in a heavy-based saucepan over a high heat and add 1 teaspoon cumin seeds and 2 teaspoons finely chopped fresh root ginger. When the ginger browns, add 2 teaspoons ground coriander, ½ teaspoon cayenne pepper and ½ teaspoon garam masala. Stir this mixture into the cooked lentils, while they are still hot, then serve.

MAKING PANEER

This is a cottage cheese made by curdling milk. The cheese can then be refrigerated to be eaten within three or four days. Rich in protein, paneer is made a lot in vegetarian homes to be used as a base for both savoury and sweet dishes.

Cottage cheese or ricotta cheese can be used as substitutes for paneer. Citric acid is sold in crystal form in at chemist shops.

To make about 150 g (5 oz), mix together 4 tablespoons lemon or 2 tablespoons lime juice or 1 teaspoon citric acid and 60 ml (2 fl oz) water in a bowl, then set aside. Line a sieve with muslin and place it over another

bowl. Bring 1 litre (35 fl oz) whole milk to the boil in a heavy-based pan over a medium heat.

When the milk boils, lower the heat and gradually stir in the juice and water mixture. The milk should start to curdle and the water, or whey, will separate from the curds. As soon as the separated water is clear and no longer milky, stop adding liquid. If the water clears before all the sour solution has been added, throw away any extra solution. If you have used all the sour solution and the water is still not clear, make up more solution and add it gradually.

Strain the curds and whey through the muslin-lined sieve, then leave to drain for at least 1 hour. The cheese left in the cloth is paneer, which will keep for 3 to 4 days in a covered container in the fridge. The liquid in the bowl can be thrown away or used for cooking rice, vegetables or lentils, or for flavouring sauces.

COOKING POPPADUMS

You are probably familiar with these paper-thin, crisp rounds from your favourite Indian restaurant. Made from lentil flour, dried poppadums are sold in supermarkets or Asian shops and are either cooked over a flame, grilled or fried.

Because they are so thin, they take hardly any time at all to cook, so it is worth having several packets in the cupboard. Just follow the cooking instructions that are printed on the back of the packet.

I like to serve poppadums as a snack with a small bowl of finely chopped onions, sprinkled with salt, lemon juice and finely chopped coriander leaves.

They are also good brushed with melted ghee flavoured with a little chilli powder when they are freshly roasted and still hot.

GOAN-STYLE CHICKEN CURRY

Combdi Che Nalla Chi Kodi

Time to make: 30 minutes
Time to cook: 30 to 40 minutes
Serves 4 to 6

1 chicken, about 1 kg (2 lb)
2 or 3 fresh green chillies
60 ml (2 fl oz) vegetable oil
250 g (8 oz) onions, grated
14 to 16 fresh curry leaves or 1 teaspoon dried and crushed
250 g (8 oz) tomatoes, very finely chopped
1½ tablespoons salt
1 teaspoon turmeric
1 teaspoon garam masala
75 g (2½ oz) creamed coconut
22 g (¾ oz) tamarind pulp, soaked in 4 tablespoons water and strained
1 tablespoon tomato ketchup
coriander leaves, to garnish

For the paste

155 g (5 oz) fresh coconut or 45 g (1½ oz) desiccated
2 tablespoons cumin seeds
2 tablespoons coriander seeds
1 tablespoon poppy seeds
2 to 4 whole dried red chillies
2 teaspoons chopped garlic
2 teaspoons chopped ginger

Menu1: Goan-style Chicken, above, served with Cucumber and Peanut Salad, see page 22, and Cabbage with Mustard Seeds, see page 23.

Adding the ketchup to this rich coconut gravy, instead of tomato purée, as one might expect, is an inspired touch that comes from my parents' cook, Sailor. He only let me in on this secret after my first book had been published when he thought I had earned the right to know!

1   Begin by making the paste. Peel the fresh coconut so you have 140 g (4½ oz) flesh. Grate the coconut. If you are using desiccated, soak it in water to cover for 30 minutes.
2   Put the cumin, coriander and poppy seeds and chillies in a dry heavy-based frying pan or wok over a high heat and toast, stirring constantly, until they turn light brown. Immediately pour the seeds and chillies out of the pan. Set aside to cool.
3   Put the roasted seeds, red chillies, grated or reconstituted coconut, garlic and ginger in a blender or food processor and process until a fine paste forms.
4   Skin the chicken and cut it into 6 pieces. Slit the chillies.
5   Heat the oil a heavy-based saucepan over a medium heat, then add the grated onions and curry leaves and stir-fry for 4 to 5 minutes until the onions are golden. Stir in the tomatoes and continue stir-frying for 8 to 10 minutes until the fat separates.
6   Stir in the coconut paste, salt, turmeric and garam masala and continue stir-frying for about 3 minutes until the mixture sticks to the pan a little. Increase the heat to high, then stir in the chicken and green chillies and cook, stirring occasionally, for about 5 minutes until the chicken is opaque.
7   Stir in 500 ml (16 fl oz) water and bring to the boil, stirring occasionally, uncovered. When the mixture boils, cover the pan, lower the heat to low and simmer for 10 to 15 minutes until all the chicken pieces are cooked through and the juices run clear.
8   Stir in the creamed coconut, diluted tamarind pulp and tomato ketchup. Return to the boil, then simmer, stirring occasionally, for 5 minutes. Transfer to a dish and garnish with chopped coriander and whole leaves.

CUCUMBER AND PEANUT SALAD
Khira Moongphali Cachoomber

Time to make: 5 minutes
Serves 4 to 6

30 g (1 oz) shelled roasted peanuts

500 g (1 lb) cucumbers

1 heaped tablespoon chopped fresh coriander leaves

1 tablespoon finely chopped seeded fresh green chillies

2 teaspoons lime juice or 4 teaspoons lemon juice

1½ teaspoons salt

½ teaspoon ground pepper

The nuts in this salad give it a unique flavour. This originates from the western regions where there is an abundance of peanuts. I first tried this when I visited my aunt, who had lived in Nagpur for a number of years. I absolutely love this and wish peanuts were not so fattening so I could eat it more often.

1   Rub the peanuts in a tea towel to remove the papery brown skins, then finely chop them. Finely dice the cucumbers.
2   Combine all the ingredients in a bowl, stirring until well blended together. Cover and refrigerate until ready to serve. Transfer to a serving bowl.

PLAIN BOILED RICE
Saade Chawal

Time to make: 30 minutes
    soaking
Time to cook: 15 minutes
Serves 4 to 6

250 g (8 oz) long-grain rice, preferably basmati

1 teaspoon lemon juice

Most Indian families eat plain rice at least once a day, and in my house it is a regular feature of the lunchtime meal. When my daughter is visiting, we usually sit down for her favourite meal – plain boiled rice and Yellow Lentils, see page 77.

1   Put the rice in a fine sieve and rinse under running cold water until the water runs clear. Transfer to a bowl with enough water to cover and leave to soak for 30 minutes.
2   Drain the rice. Place the rice, lemon juice and 625 ml (20 fl oz) water in a heavy-based saucepan over a high heat and bring to the boil, uncovered, then cover the pan, lower the heat to low and simmer for about 10 minutes until all the water is absorbed and the grains are tender. Transfer to a serving dish and serve.

CABBAGE WITH MUSTARD SEEDS
Patta Gobhi

Time to make: 5 minutes
Time to cook: 3 minutes
Serves 4 to 6

500 g (1 lb) green cabbage

60 ml (2 fl oz) vegetable oil

1 teaspoon mustard seeds

2 or 3 dried red chillies

2 teaspoons salt

1 tablespoon lemon juice

2 tablespoons chopped fresh coriander leaves, to garnish

I like this for its crunchy texture and the combination of mustard seeds and chillies together. If you chill this before serving, it makes an excellent salad.

1 Remove the core from the cabbage, then finely shred the leaves.
2 Heat the oil in a heavy-based saucepan or wok over a high heat, then stir in the mustard seeds and dried red chillies.
3 When the seeds splutter, stir in the cabbage and salt and stir-fry for 3 to 4 minutes until the cabbage is just tender.
4 Turn off heat and stir in lemon juice, stirring until everything is well blended together. Transfer to a serving dish and garnish with chopped coriander. Serve immediately.

Variation
You can cook the cabbage with Tomato Masala, see page 10, or Red Masala, see page 10. When the masala is ready and the fat separates, add the finely shredded cabbage and stir-fry, over a high heat, until just tender.

CHICKEN WITH COCONUT AND SPICES

Combdi Xacuti

Time to make: 30 minutes
Time to cook: 30 minutes
Serves 4 to 6

---

375 g (12 oz) onions

140 g (4½ oz) fresh coconut or 75 g (2½ oz) desiccated

125 ml (4 fl oz) vegetable oil

½ teaspoon black cumin seeds

8 black peppercorns

8 cloves

1 tablespoon fennel seeds

1 tablespoon coriander seeds

2 teaspoons broken cinnamon stick, or ½ teaspoon ground

1 chicken, about 1 kg (2 lb)

4 tablespoons chopped fresh coriander

fresh coriander sprigs and lemon wedges to garnish

Menu 2: Chicken with Coconut and Spices, above, served with Lemon Rice, see page 26, Spiced Beans and a Wholemeal Paratha, both on page 27.

Another Goan dish made with exotic spices and coconut. I had my first version of this in an eating shack on the beach at Goa. I liked it so much that I asked my friend Lalita for a recipe. Now I make it for entertaining in Delhi because it is so unusual here and it's always popular. If you make this with boneless chicken cubes, instead of whole pieces, it is good served as a snack.

1   Roughly chop the onions and set aside. If you are using fresh coconut, peel it so you have 125 g (4 oz) flesh, then grate the flesh. If you are using desiccated, put it in a bowl with water to cover and leave to soak for 30 minutes. Drain well.

2   Heat the oil in a heavy-based, deep frying pan or flameproof casserole over a high heat, then add the black cumin seeds, peppercorns, cloves, fennel and coriander seeds and cinnamon. When the seeds splutter, stir in the chopped onions and stir-fry until they become transparent. Stir in coconut and continue stir-frying for about 2 minutes until the mixture becomes brown. Turn off the heat and leave mixture to cool slightly.

3   Transfer the mixture to a blender or food processor and process until a fine paste forms. Meanwhile, skin the chicken and cut it into 6 pieces.

4   Transfer the paste back to the frying pan or flameproof casserole over a high heat and heat through, stirring. Stir in the chicken pieces and cook, stirring, for about 5 minutes until they become opaque.

5   Cover the pan, lower the heat and simmer for about 15 minutes until all the chicken pieces are cooked through and the juices run clear when each piece is pierced. There should be very little liquid left and the chicken pieces should be coated with the mixture. If this has not happened, continue simmering, uncovered, until all liquid evaporates.

6   Stir in half the chopped coriander. Transfer to a serving dish and sprinkle with the remaining coriander. Garnish with coriander sprigs and lemon wedges. Serve immediately.

LEMON RICE
Nimbu Bhaat

Time to make: 5 minutes, plus
 30 minutes soaking
Time to cook: 15 minutes
Serves 4 to 6

**250 g (8 oz) long-grain rice,
preferably basmati**

2 tablespoons vegetable oil

large pinch ground asafoetida

1 teaspoon mustard seeds

**7 to 8 fresh curry leaves or
½ teaspoon dried and crushed**

2 or 3 whole dried red chillies

2 teaspoons salt

½ teaspoon turmeric

2 tablespoons lemon juice

**2 tablespoons chopped fresh
coriander leaves**

Lemon gives this rice dish a very refreshing flavour, and I often eat this with just yogurt as an accompaniment. I always used to ask a friend to make this for me when I would visit, then finally I realised how easy it is to make. It looks pretty, and you can add extra lemon or spices if you want a more pronounced flavour. This dish is popular in the southern and western regions of India.

1   Put the rice in a fine sieve and rinse under running cold water the until water runs clear.
2   Put the rice and enough water to cover in a bowl and leave the rice to soak for 30 minutes.
3   Drain the rice. Heat the oil in a heavy-based saucepan over a high heat, then add the ground asafoetida, mustard seeds, curry leaves and red chillies.
4   When the seeds splutter, add the rice, stirring to coat all the grains in oil. Stir in the salt, turmeric and 625 ml (20 fl oz) water and bring to the boil, uncovered.
5   When the water boils, add a few drops of the lemon juice, cover the pan, lower the heat to low and simmer for about 10 minutes until all the water is absorbed and the grains are tender.
6   Remove from the heat and stir in the remaining lemon juice and half the coriander. Transfer to a serving dish and garnish with the remaining coriander. Serve immediately.

SPICED BEANS
Frans Beans

Time to make: 5 minutes
Time to cook: about 10 minutes
Serves 4 to 6

500 g (1 lb) French beans
60 ml (2 fl oz) vegetable oil
1 teaspoon mustard seeds
2 or 3 whole dried red chillies
2 teaspoons salt
1 tablespoon lemon juice
chopped fresh coriander, to garnish

Green beans are popular all over India. You can make the recipe as I suggest here, or add finely chopped carrots.

1 Top and tail the beans, then chop them.
2 Heat the oil in a heavy-based saucepan or wok over a high heat, then stir in the mustard seeds and dried red chillies. When the seeds splutter, stir in beans and salt and stir-fry for 5 to 8 minutes until beans are just tender.
3 Turn off the heat and stir in the lemon juice until blended. Transfer to a serving dish and garnish with chopped coriander.

WHOLEMEAL PARATHAS

If you are in a hurry, by all means buy ready-baked parathas from Indian shops or large supermarkets. If you have time, however, I think it is worth the effort of making them yourself.

Place 315 g (10 oz) plain wholemeal flour in a deep bowl and make a well in the centre. Pour in 60 ml (2 fl oz) water and gradually mix together, adding an extra 60 ml (2 fl oz) water or enough to form a sticky dough. Roll dough around bowl to pick up all the flour from sides, then knead until it is soft and smooth. Your fingers should be able to press into dough with hardly any pressure.

Shape dough into a ball and put back in bowl. Cover with a damp towel and leave for at least 30 minutes. Meanwhile, melt 125 g (4 oz) ghee.

Knead dough a little, then form into a long roll. Break off 8 equal-sized pieces. Roll pieces into smooth balls, dusting with a little flour if sticky. Roll out each ball into a round about 0.5 cm (¼ in) thick.

Brush ghee over a rolled-out round, fold in half, then smear with more ghee and fold into quarters. Roll out as thinly as possible. Repeat with all dough balls, covering each with a cloth as you roll them out. The ultimate is to be fast enough to roll one and fry another at the same time, but that takes a bit of practice!

Heat a griddle or *tawa* over a high heat until if a drop of water is thrown over, it will evaporate immediately with a sizzling sound. Cook one paratha at a time until edges start rising. Put some ghee in a spoon and quickly make a trail along outer edge, so some trickles under; smear extra ghee on top.

When underside is golden, increase heat and turn paratha over using tongs. Lower heat and cook until it is golden brown. Serve at once.

BUTTER CHICKEN
Murgh Makhani

Time to make: 5 minutes
Time to cook: 10 to 15 minutes
Serves 4 to 6

1 shop-bought tandoori chicken, about 1 kg (2 lb)
30 g (1 oz) butter
1 teaspoon vegetable oil
1 teaspoon black cumin seeds
250 g (8 oz) tomato purée
2 teaspoons salt
185 ml (6 fl oz) single cream
1 fresh green chilli, thinly sliced lengthways, to garnish

With its creamy tomato gravy, I think this is an interesting variation of tandoori chicken. Until I was about 18 years old I was a strict vegetarian, and this was one of the first meat dishes I would eat. I started my conversion slowly by just eating the gravy and then I graduated to eating the pieces of chicken.

You can, of course, make your own tandoori chicken, see page 38, but here I suggest using a shop-bought one because it is so much quicker. If you want to make this in advance, stir in the cream and turn off the heat. Leave the mixture to cool, then cover and refrigerate until required. You can then re-heat it just before serving.

1   Cut the chicken into 6 or 8 pieces.
2   Melt the butter with the oil in a heavy-based frying pan or wok over a medium heat, then stir in the black cumin seeds and tomato purée. Continue stirring until the mixture comes to the boil and the tomato purée splutters.
3   When the tomato purée splutters, stir in the salt and chicken pieces, stirring occasionally until all pieces are well coated and heated through, 5 to 10 minutes.
4   Stir in the cream and continue cooking over a medium heat for 2 minutes until blended and the chicken and sauce are hot. Transfer to a serving dish and garnish with sliced green chilli. Serve immediately.

Menu 3: Butter Chicken, above, served with Cucumber Raita and Pickled Onions, both on page 30, and Naans, see page 47.

PICKLED ONIONS

Sirke Wala Pyaaz

Time to make: 10 to 15 minutes,
    plus cooling
Serves 4 to 6

10 to 12 pickling onions, about 250 g (8 oz)

250 ml (8 fl oz) malt vinegar

1 teaspoon sugar

1 teaspoon salt

Cook's Tip
Like most other pickles, these are good served with all meals. I make these twice a year, so I always have them on hand for a quick meal like this one. These are ready to eat straight away, or you can store them in a cool, dark place for up to 8 months.

It's interesting to see how the onions I make this with in India turn pink as soon as you put them into the vinegar. As a child, I liked going to a particular restaurant because they served these. I always wondered how the colour was injected into them!

1   Peel the onions, then rinse them in a colander under running cold water. Set aside to drain.
2   Bring the vinegar to the boil in a heavy-based saucepan or wok over a high heat. Stir in the sugar, salt and onions, stirring until sugar and salt dissolve. Bring the vinegar to the boil again, then remove from the heat and leave the onions and liquid to cool. When cool, transfer to sterilised, airtight jars.

CUCUMBER RAITA

Khire Ka Raita

Time to make: 10 minutes
Serves 4 to 6

500 g (1 lb) cucumbers

440 g (14 oz) plain yogurt

2 tablespoons chopped fresh coriander

2 teaspoons ground cumin

2 teaspoons salt

¼ teaspoon ground black pepper

¼ teaspoon cayenne pepper

mint sprig, to garnish

1   Peel and grate the cucumbers. Put the yogurt in a bowl and beat until it is smooth, adding a little water to make a thick pouring consistency.
2   Stir in the coriander and half the ground cumin, the salt and black pepper. Use your hands to squeeze all the excess moisture from the cucumber and stir it in.
3   Transfer to a serving bowl and garnish with the remaining ground cumin, the cayenne pepper and a mint sprig.

NORTHERN-STYLE CHICKEN CURRY

Murgh Rasedar

Time to make: 15 minutes
Time to cook: 20 to 30 minutes
Serves 4 to 6

1 chicken, about 1 kg (2 lb)

2 tablespoons single cream, optional

2 tablespoons chopped fresh coriander leaves, to garnish

For the masala

500 g (1 lb) onions

315 g (10 oz) tomatoes

1 tablespoon peeled and chopped fresh root ginger

1 tablespoon chopped garlic

60 ml (2 fl oz) vegetable oil

1 tablespoon cumin seeds

4 bay leaves

2 tablespoons ground coriander

1 tablespoon salt

2 teaspoons garam masala, see page 9

½ teaspoon turmeric

½ teaspoon chilli powder

*R*asedar means gravied, and this is an example of a typical gravied chicken dish from northern India. Make the gravy thick or thin to suit your taste by adding more or less water than I suggest. It took me a long time to master how long to cook the masala to get the correct taste. Curries in all Indian households taste different because the masalas are cooked for varying times. After I tried many styles, I decided that cooking the masala until it was medium brown was what I liked the most.

If you want to experiment, adding chopped fenugreek or spinach leaves with the chicken will produce a different flavour.

1 Begin by making the masala. Roughly chop the onions and finely chop the tomatoes. Put the ginger, garlic and onions in a blender or food processor and process until a smooth paste forms.
2 Heat the oil in a heavy-based saucepan or flameproof casserole over a high heat, then add the cumin seeds and bay leaves. When the seeds splutter, stir in the onion paste and stir-fry until it turns light brown. Stir in the tomatoes and continue stir-frying until all liquid evaporates and the fat separates.
3 Stir in the ground coriander, salt, garam masala, turmeric and chilli powder, stirring until well blended.
4 Meanwhile, skin the chicken and cut it into 6 pieces. Stir the chicken pieces into the masala and cook, stirring occasionally, for about 5 minutes until they are well coated and become opaque.
5 Stir in 375 ml (12 fl oz) water and bring to the boil, stirring occasionally, uncovered. Lower the heat and simmer, uncovered, for about 15 minutes until the chicken is cooked through and juices run clear when each piece is pierced with a knife.
6 Transfer to a serving dish, spoon the cream over if you are using, and garnish with chopped coriander.

CAULIFLOWER WITH POTATOES
Gobhi Aloo

Time to make: 10 minutes
Time to cook: about 35 minutes
Serves 4 to 6

---

500 g (1 lb) cauliflower

250 g (8 oz) potatoes

2 or 3 fresh green chillies

60 ml (2 fl oz) vegetable oil

1 teaspoon cumin seeds

**1 tablespoon finely sliced
peeled fresh root ginger**

2 teaspoons salt

1 tablespoon ground coriander

½ teaspoon chilli powder

½ teaspoon garam masala

½ teaspoon turmeric

**chopped fresh coriander leaves
and fresh mint leaves,
to garnish**

A very popular dish during the winter months in northern India when fresh and tender cauliflower is plentiful. In fact, I know many of my friends say they tire of this dish during the winter, but I never do. If I am having lunch alone, I will have this with plain yogurt and Ginger and Lemon Relish, see page 16. This is lightly spiced and is a good accompaniment to most gravied dishes.

1 Begin by preparing the vegetables. Break the cauliflower into florets and cut the potatoes into pieces about the same size as the florets. Slit each of the chillies lengthways.

2 Heat the oil in a heavy-based saucepan or flameproof casserole over a high heat, then add the cumin seeds.

3 When the seeds splutter, stir in the ginger and stir-fry until it becomes light brown.

4 Add the cauliflower florets, potatoes and chillies, stirring to coat all the pieces in oil. Stir in the salt, ground coriander, chilli powder, garam masala and turmeric and continue stir-frying until well blended together.

5 Cover the pan, lower the heat and simmer, stirring occasionally, for about 30 minutes until the vegetables are just tender. Transfer to a serving dish and garnish with chopped coriander and fresh mint. Serve immediately.

Menu 4: Northern-style Chicken Curry, see page 31, served with Cauliflower with Potatoes, above, and Plain Boiled Rice, see page 22.

GRILLED CHICKEN WITH SESAME SEEDS

Murgh - E - Til

Time to make: 10 minutes, plus
    marinating
Time to cook: about 20 minutes
Serves 4 to 6

---

30 g (1 oz) white sesame seeds

1½ teaspoons chopped garlic

**1½ teaspoons chopped
peeled fresh root ginger**

1 chicken, about 1 kg (2 lb)

125 g (4 oz) plain yogurt

**1 tablespoon chopped fresh
green chillies**

**1 tablespoon chopped fresh
coriander leaves**

2 teaspoons salt

**lemon wedges and thin onion
slices, to garnish**

Variation
This is a versatile recipe that can
easily be adapted for different
meals. Use the marinade to flavour
prawns, fish or paneer, see page 19,
and then grill as in this recipe.

A delicious sesame-flavoured dish with a crunchy texture that
can be prepared ahead of time and then refrigerated until
you are ready to grill it. You can also use boneless pieces of
chicken if you like. I thought of the idea for this recipe when I
was eating Chinese-style sesame prawn toasts. This is a real hit
when I entertain because the combination of grilled chicken and
sesame seeds isn't that common in Delhi.

1   Heat a dry heavy-based frying pan or wok over a high heat
and toast the sesame seeds, stirring constantly, until they are light
brown. Immediately pour the seeds out of the pan to stop the
toasting. Set aside.
2   Put the garlic and ginger in a mortar and use the pestle to
pound together to form a smooth paste.
3   Skin the chicken and cut it into 6 pieces. Prick each piece of
chicken in 2 or 3 places with a fork. Put the chicken, toasted
sesame seeds, garlic and ginger paste, yogurt, green chillies,
chopped coriander and salt in a bowl and stir together until well
blended and all the chicken pieces are coated. Cover and
marinate in the fridge for at least 3 or 4 hours, or overnight.
4   Set the grill to high. Place the chicken pieces on a wire rack
over a baking sheet to catch drips and grill for about 20 minutes
until all the pieces are cooked through and the juices run clear
when each piece is pierced with the tip of a knife.
5   Transfer to a serving plate and garnish with lemon wedges for
squeezing over each portion and onion rings. Serve immediately.

Cook's Tip
I prefer to grill the chicken in a grill that has heating elements on
the top and bottom, so it isn't necessary to turn the chicken
pieces over. If you don't have a grill like this, I think it is better
to bake the pieces on a wire rack over a baking tray at 200C,
425F, Gas 7.

*Menu 5: Grilled Chicken with
Sesame Seeds, above, served with
Paneer with Onions and Tomatoes,
see page 36, and Onion Relish with
Mint, see page 37.*

PANEER WITH ONIONS AND TOMATOES

Paneer Ki Bhurji

Time to make: 5 minutes, plus
   making the paneer
Time to cook: 8 to 10 minutes
Serves 4 to 6

---

125 g (4 oz) onions

---

125 g (4 oz) tomatoes

---

2 fresh green chillies

---

500 g (1 lb) paneer, see page 19

---

2 tablespoons vegetable oil

---

1 teaspoon cumin seeds

---

2 teaspoons salt

---

2 teaspoons ground coriander

½ teaspoon garam masala, see page 9

½ teaspoon chilli powder

¼ teaspoon turmeric

Here is one of the quickest recipes I know of for cooking paneer. *Bhurji* means scrambled, which makes an appropriate title for this dish because the paneer does get scrambled while it cooks. Consequently, this is a good dish to make if you make paneer and it doesn't turn out as set as it should be. If the idea of scrambled paneer doesn't appeal, you can grate the paneer before you add it to the pan.

1 Thickly slice the onions and chop the tomatoes. Cut a long slit in each of the chillies. Make sure the paneer is well drained, then cut it into cubes.

2 Heat the oil in a heavy-based frying pan or wok over a high heat, then add the cumin seeds.

3 When the seeds splutter, stir in the sliced onions and stir-fry until they look fried but do not change colour.

4 Stir in the chopped tomatoes and slit green chillies and continue stir-frying until they also look fried but do not change colour. Add the salt, ground coriander, garam masala, chilli powder and turmeric, stirring until well blended together.

5 Stir in the cubed paneer and heat through, stirring occasionally. Transfer to a serving dish. Serve immediately.

ONION RELISH WITH MINT

Poodine ki Chutney

Time to make: 10 minutes
Makes about 220 g (7 oz)

1 teaspoon cumin seeds
125 g (4 oz) fresh mint sprigs
125 g (4 oz) onions
2 teaspoons pomegranate seeds
2 teaspoons salt
2 tablespoons chopped green chillies
2 teaspoons sugar

The mint is very refreshing and the sourness of the pomegranate seeds is very distinctive in this exceptionally quick and easy relish. Like Coriander Chutney, see page 44, this can also be served as part of a meal or with snacks; both chutneys are interchangeable.

1 Toast the cumin seeds in a dry heavy-based frying pan or wok over a high heat, stirring constantly, until they turn dark brown. Immediately pour the seeds out of the pan to stop the toasting and set aside to cool.
2 Tear the mint leaves off the stalks. Discard the tough stalks but you can keep the tender stalks that break easily with a snap.
3 Put all the ingredients in a blender or food processor and process until a fine paste forms. Keep in a covered container in the fridge for up to one week.

Variations
If you would like a thinner consistency, add some plain yogurt after processing.

You can also substitute 2 tablespoons lemon juice or 60 g (2 oz) grated raw mango for the pomegranate seeds.

TANDOORI CHICKEN
Tandoori Murghi

Time to make: 10 minutes, plus marinating
Time to cook: about 20 minutes
Serves 4 to 6

1 chicken, about 1 kg (2 lb)

1 onion, thinly sliced, to garnish

lemon wedges and coriander sprigs, to garnish

For the Tandoori Masala

2 tablespoons chopped garlic

2 tablespoons chopped peeled fresh root ginger

3 tablespoons malt vinegar, or 220 g (7 oz) plain yogurt

1 tablespoon salt

2 teaspoons chilli powder

1 teaspoon garam masala, see page 9

½ teaspoon ground fenugreek

1 teaspoon chaat ka masala, see page 9

1 teaspoon freshly ground black pepper

few drops red food colouring, optional

Although this universally popular dish appears time consuming to make, it is actually quite quick once you have the tandoori masala to hand. If you make up the masala and leave the chicken to marinate overnight it can then be put in the oven without any fuss while you prepare the other quick dishes. This recipe is also delicious for grilling or cooking on a barbecue.

1   Begin by making the tandoori masala. Put the garlic and ginger in a mortar and use the pestle to pound together to form a smooth paste. Alternatively, use the side of a wide-bladed knife to pound them together.

2   Put the garlic and ginger paste, vinegar or yogurt, salt, chilli powder, garam masala, ground fenugreek, chaat ka masala, black pepper and food colouring, if desired, in a large bowl and stir until well blended together.

3   Skin the chicken, then prick it all over with a fork. Add the chicken to the bowl and use your hands to rub the tandoori masala into the flesh. Cover the bowl and marinate in the fridge for at least 4 to 6 hours, or overnight, turning the chicken over several times.

4   Set the oven to 220C, 425F, Gas 7. Set a wire rack over a roasting pan and put the chicken on top. Bake the chicken for about 10 minutes, then turn it over and bake for another 10 minutes or until cooked through and juices run clear when thighs are pierced with tip of a knife.

5   Cut into serving pieces, if you want, then transfer to a serving dish and garnish with lemon pieces for squeezing over each portion and fresh coriander. Serve immediately.

Cook's Tip
If you make up double the masala mixture, it will keep in the fridge for 4 to 6 weeks, ready to use a second time, or for cooking fish, paneer and meat.

Menu 6: Tandoori Chicken, above, served with Spinach and Paneer, see page 40, Spiced Chick-peas and Deep-fried Bread, both on page 41.

SPINACH AND PANEER
Palak Paneer

Time to make: 15 minutes, plus making paneer and puréeing spinach
Time to cook: 20 minutes
Serves 4 to 6

500 g (1 lb) paneer, see page 19

vegetable oil for deep frying, plus 60 ml (2 fl oz) extra

1 kg (2 lb) fresh spinach or 375 g (12 oz) frozen chopped spinach, thawed

125 g (4 oz) onions

250 g (8 oz) tomatoes

60 ml (2 fl oz) vegetable oil

1 teaspoon cumin seeds

1 bay leaf

1 teaspoon finely chopped peeled fresh root ginger

1 teaspoon chopped garlic

2 teaspoons salt

1 teaspoon ground coriander

½ teaspoon chilli powder

¼ teaspoon garam masala, see page 9

1 long dried red chilli, lightly fried, to garnish

With the off-white colour of the paneer and the green of the spinach, this dish is as colourful as it is flavourful. I know some cooks who like to add the paneer unfried, but I think the method I use here is much tastier.

1   Make sure the paneer is well drained, then cut into bite-sized pieces. Heat the vegetable oil in a deep, heavy-based frying pan or a flameproof casserole over a high heat and add the paneer. Fry until it is lightly browned on all sides, then turn it over carefully with a wooden spoon so you don't break it up. Drain it well on paper towels and set aside.

2   If you are using fresh spinach, cut out the thick stalks and rinse the leaves well, then finely chop them. If you are using frozen spinach make sure it is thawed, then squeeze it with your hands to remove all the excess moisture. Put the fresh or frozen spinach in a blender or food processor and process until smooth. Set aside.

3   Grate the onions and finely chop the tomatoes.

4   Heat 60 ml (2 fl oz) vegetable oil in a heavy-based saucepan over a high heat, then add the cumin seeds.

5   When the seeds splutter, add the bay leaf, ginger and garlic and stir-fry until they turn light brown. Stir in the chopped onions and continue stir-frying for about 1 minute until they turn golden brown.

6   Lower the heat to medium, then stir in the finely chopped tomatoes and continue stir-frying for 2 to 3 minutes until the fat separates. Add the salt, ground coriander, chilli powder and garam masala, stirring until well blended together.

7   Add the puréed spinach and continue cooking, stirring occasionally, for 2 to 3 minutes, then stir in the paneer and cook until heated through. Transfer to a serving dish and garnish with a fried chilli. Serve immediately.

SPICED CHICK-PEAS

Pindi Channas

Time to make: 30 minutes
Time to cook: about 10 minutes
Serves 4 to 6

1 tablespoon loose tea leaves

three 440 g (14 oz) cans
chick-peas

3 or 4 fresh green chillies

2 large potatoes

2 tablespoons ground coriander

1 tablespoon ground
pomegranate seeds

1 tablespoon roasted and
ground cumin

1 teaspoon garam masala, see
page 9

1 teaspoon ground black
pepper

1 tablespoon salt

185 ml (6 fl oz) vegetable oil

2 tablespoons finely shredded
peeled fresh root ginger

This is a childhood favourite of my siblings and myself with the *bhaturas*. We still like the combination, and if none of us feels like cooking we will get together at a specific restaurant where we can enjoy both dishes. The unique feature of this highly spiced recipe is that the chick-peas are cooked with tea leaves to give them a darker colour. I also like to serve this with lemon quarters for squeezing over each portion.

1   Put the tea leaves in the centre of a piece of muslin and tie up to make a pouch. Cook the chick-peas and their liquid with the tea leaves for 5 minutes, then turn off the heat and leave for at least 15 minutes so they absorb colour.

2   Meanwhile, slit each of the green chillies and set aside. Cube the potatoes and put them in a large saucepan of water and bring to the boil, then cook for about 10 minutes or until tender. Drain well and set aside.

3   Put the chick-peas and the liquid, coriander, ground pomegranate seeds, cumin, garam masala, black pepper and salt in a bowl and stir until blended.

4   Heat the oil in a heavy-based saucepan or wok over a high heat and stir-fry the ginger until it is light brown. Stir in the chillies and potatoes, then the chick-pea mixture and continue stirring until lightly fried and blended. Serve immediately.

DEEP-FRIED BREAD
Bhatura

I had to try this recipe many times before I got the *bhaturas* to turn out like they do at my favourite restaurant. But once I learned the secret, I realised how easy they are! Just be careful not to make the dough too soft to roll out. Also, stop adding the water as soon as the dough forms.

Place 315 g(10 oz) plain and 250 g (8 oz) wholemeal flours in a bowl. Stir in 1 teaspoon salt, 1 teaspoon baking soda and about 250 g (8 oz) plain yogurt. Slowly add water if necessary until a soft dough forms.

Lightly knead dough in bowl until soft and smooth. Your finger should be able to press in with hardly any pressure. Shape dough into a ball and place in bowl. Cover with a damp cloth and leave to rise in a warm, draught-free place until doubled in size, 2 to 3 hours, depending on the temperature .

Knock back dough and break it up into 20 to 25 walnut-size pieces. Roll into smooth balls, then roll out thinly into rounds on a lightly floured surface with a floured rolling pin.

Heat about 5 cm (2 in) vegetable oil in a wok over a high heat until a small piece of dough thrown in comes back up to the surface immediately. Fry *bhaturas* one at a time until lightly brown on each side. Drain well and keep warm until all are fried. Serve hot.

YOGURT CHICKEN

Kalmi Murgh

Time to make: 10 minutes
Time to cook: about 20 minutes,
  plus grilling
Serves 4 to 6

1 chicken, about 1 kg (2 lb)
1 tablespoon chopped garlic
1 tablespoon chopped peeled fresh root ginger
220 g (7 oz) plain yogurt
1 tablespoon salt
2 cloves
½ teaspoon broken cinnamon stick, or ⅛ teaspoon ground
2 tablespoons lime juice or 4 tablespoons lemon juice
approximately 125 g (4 oz) plain flour
1 tablespoon chopped fresh mint leaves, to garnish
1 large onion, thinly sliced, to garnish
1 lemon, cut into wedges, to garnish

I had to visit a particular restaurant about ten times until I could make this dish just the way I wanted it at home, and finally my family banned the place because they had had enough of this! But I think it was worth the effort in the end, and so will you after you have tried this delectable dish.

1   Cut the chicken into 6 pieces and set aside in a heavy-based saucepan. Put the garlic and ginger in a mortar and use the pestle to pound together to form a smooth paste. Alternatively, use the side of a wide-bladed knife to pound them together.
2   Add the garlic and ginger paste, yogurt, salt, cloves and cinnamon to the chicken and stir to coat all the pieces in the masala mixture. Bring to the boil, then lower the heat and simmer, stirring occasionally, until all the liquid evaporates and the chicken is cooked through and juices run clear when each piece is pierced with the tip of a knife. If the chicken is cooked through before all liquid evaporates, remove the pieces and continue cooking the mixture over a high heat, stirring occasionally. In any case, take care that the chicken is not so well cooked that it starts to fall off the bones.
3   Turn off the heat, then stir in the lime or lemon juice and leave the chicken to cool.
4   Set the grill to high or the oven to 220C, 425F, Gas 7. Put the flour on a plate, then dredge the chicken pieces in flour, shaking off any excess.
5   Grill the chicken pieces until light brown, turning them several times, or bake for about 10 minutes until heated through. Transfer to a serving plate and garnish with chopped mint, onion slices and lemon wedges for squeezing over each portion.

Cook's Tip
To save time, you can prepare the chicken through step 3 and then refrigerate it overnight, so all that is left to do is the final grilling or baking and then it is ready to serve.

Menu 7: Yogurt Chicken, above, served with Stuffed Okra and Coriander Chutney, both on page 44.

CORIANDER CHUTNEY
Hara Dhania Chutney

Time to make: 10 minutes
Makes about 75 g (2½ oz)

30 g (1 oz) fresh green chillies
100 g (3½ oz) fresh coriander
6 to 8 cloves garlic
14 to 16 fresh curry leaves or 1 teaspoon dried and crushed
2 tablespoons lemon juice
2 teaspoons salt

This refreshing combination of fresh coriander leaves and spices is used to accompany food, much as pickles are used in Western homes. This particular recipe is good with samosas, which can be bought with meat or vegetarian fillings.

1   Remove the seeds from the chillies and chop the flesh.
2   Put all the ingredients in a blender or food processor and process together. Add a little water only if the chutney is too stiff. Transfer to a serving dish and garnish with lime slices. Serve immediately. This will keep in the fridge for 15 to 20 days.

STUFFED OKRA
Sabut Bhindi

Time to make: 20 minutes
Time to cook: about 20 minutes
Serves 4 to 6

500 g (1 lb) okra
60 ml (2 fl oz) vegetable oil
1 tablespoon lemon juice

For the masala mixture

1 tablespoon each salt, ground coriander, ground cumin, dried mango powder and chilli powder
½ teaspoon each turmeric and ground ginger
pinch ground asafoetida

I like this because the okra stays a bit crunchy. For a packed lunch or a snack, roll up these okras inside chapatis.

1   Rinse the okra and pat them dry with kitchen paper. Slice off the tops of the okra, then cut off the pointed tips. Slit each okra lengthways to make an opening to stuff.
2   Stir all the masala ingredients in a bowl. Use a round-bladed knife to stuff each okra with the masala.
3   Heat the oil in a large wok or frying pan over a high heat, then add the stuffed okra. Stir-fry for 3 to 4 minutes until glossy.
4   Lower the heat to medium, then add 1 teaspoon of the lemon juice and continue cooking, uncovered. Add the remaining lemon juice in 2 stages and continue stir-frying for about 10 minutes or until the okra are tender but still bright green and have retained their shape. Transfer to a serving dish. Serve immediately.

LAMB WITH ONION AND SPICES

Ishtoo

Time to make: 10 to 15 minutes
Time to cook: about 1 hour
Serves 4 to 6

---

500 g (1 lb) boneless leg of lamb

500 g (1 lb) onions

2 teaspoons chopped garlic

1 tablespoon chopped peeled fresh root ginger

125 ml (4 fl oz) vegetable oil

2 teaspoons cumin seeds

4 black peppercorns

3 or 4 cloves

2 bay leaves

1 large cardamom pod

60 g (2 oz) tomatoes

125 g (4 oz) plain yogurt

1 tablespoon salt

1 tablespoon ground coriander

2 or 3 whole dried red chillies, to taste, plus 2 extra, lightly fried, to garnish

chopped fresh coriander leaves, to garnish

This was a favourite recipe that my family and I always enjoyed at particular wayside eating place, and I was determined to work out the recipe so I could cook it at home. The only problem was that I couldn't bring myself to include as much fat as the cooks did! Still, I think you will enjoy this slightly lighter version.

1   Cut the lamb into cubes and chop half the onions.
2   Put the onions, garlic and ginger in a blender or food processor and process until a smooth paste forms.
3   Heat the oil in a large, heavy-based saucepan over a high heat, then add the cumin seeds, black peppercorns, cloves, bay leaves and cardamom pod. When the seeds splutter, add the onion paste and stir-fry until light brown. Stir in the meat and continue stir-frying for 3 to 4 minutes until pieces turn opaque.
4   Stir in 250 ml (8 fl oz) water and bring to the boil, then cover the pan, lower the heat and simmer for about 30 minutes until the meat is almost tender.
5   Meanwhile, finely slice the remaining onions and grate the tomatoes.
6   Uncover the pan, increase the heat and stir-fry the meat for 8 to 10 minutes until the fat separates. Stir in the yogurt, 1 tablespoon at a time, then add sliced onions, grated tomatoes, salt, ground coriander and 2 or 3 whole dried red chillies, stir-frying for about 10 minutes until well blended together and the fat separates again.
7   Transfer to a serving dish and garnish with fried red chillies and chopped coriander. Serve immediately.

MUSHROOMS AND PEAS

Mattar Mushroom Sookha

Time to make: 5 minutes
Time to cook: 8 to 10 minutes
Serves 4 to 6

1 quantity Tomato Masala, see page 10

1 kg (2 lb) fresh peas or 350 g (12 oz) frozen peas, thawed

220 g (7 oz) field mushrooms

chopped coriander, to garnish

Fresh mushrooms are a recent addition to the Indian food scene and are usually cooked in vegetarian dishes with a gravy. I prefer them this way. You can substitute Red Masala, see page 10, for the Tomato Masala if you like.

1   Make the masala in a large heavy-based saucepan or wok over a medium heat, or re-heat it until the fat separates.
2   Meanwhile, shell the peas if you are using fresh ones and slice the mushrooms if they are large.
3   Add the peas and mushrooms to the masala and stir-fry until the peas are tender. Transfer to a serving dish and garnish with chopped coriander. Serve immediately.

Menu 8: Lamb with Onion and Spices, see page 45, served on Lemon Rice, see page 26, and accompanied with Mushrooms and Peas, above.

NAANS

Naans are traditionally cooked on the side of a *tandoor* oven, but are quite easy to make at home using a conventional oven or grill. Although this is a recipe for a plain naan, you can make it richer by adding ghee to the dough and smearing it with extra ghee as soon as it is baked. If you are in a hurry, speed up the rising time by putting the covered bowl with the dough into a larger container of hot water; the rising will take only about 2 hours.

Sift 500 g (1 lb) plain flour, 1 teaspoon baking soda and 1 teaspoon salt into a bowl. Stir in 250 g (8 oz) plain yogurt and mix together to form a dough. Lightly knead until soft and smooth; your finger should be able to press into the dough with hardly any pressure. Shape into a ball and place in bowl. Cover with a damp cloth and leave until doubled in size; this can take 6 hours but depends on the temperature.

Knock back the dough and knead on a lightly floured surface, adding just a little extra flour if it sticks. Shape into a ball and return to bowl. Cover and leave to rise again until doubled in size; this should take much less time.

Turn out on to a lightly floured surface and knead. Break off 6 to 8 walnut-size pieces and shape into balls. Place on a lightly floured surface, cover and leave at least 15 minutes until smooth and puffed up. Set the oven to 220C, 425F, Gas 7 and lightly grease a baking sheet.

Roll out balls on a lightly floured surface into flat oval or round shapes, stretching and pulling with your hands. Lightly brush each with a little milk or water, then sprinkle over onion seeds. Place on baking sheet and bake 5 minutes until they bubble up unevenly and have specks of brown. Remove and keep warm until all are baked. To make even richer, brush with melted ghee or butter as soon as they come out of oven.

BEEF BIRYANI

Gosht Biryani

Time to make: 30 to 45 minutes
Time to cook: 1½ hours
Serves 4 to 6

---

500 g (1 lb) onions

500 g (1 lb) lean beef, such as shoulder or leg

1 tablespoon chopped garlic

1 tablespoon chopped ginger

125 ml (4 fl oz) vegetable oil, plus 2 tablespoons extra for cooking rice

1 teaspoon black cumin seeds

220 g (7 oz) plain yogurt

1 tablespoon salt

1 teaspoon garam masala, see page 9

1 bay leaf

60 ml (2 fl oz) single cream

2 tablespoons chopped coriander

For the rice

315 g (10 oz) long-grain rice, preferably basmati

½ teaspoon black cumin seeds

2 green cardamom pods

2 cloves

1 small piece stick cinnamon, about the size of a clove, broken up, or a pinch ground

1 teaspoon salt

½ teaspoon saffron threads

2 tablespoons milk, warm

Menu 9: Beef Biryani, above, served with Potatoes and Yogurt, see page 51, and Cucumber Salad, see page 50.

A Mogul-style preparation of rice and meat which is a meal in itself. In fact, I often make this for Sunday lunch. A simple salad and yogurt are all you need to serve with this.

1   Put the rice in a fine sieve and rinse under running cold water until the water runs clear. Put the rice and enough water to cover in a bowl and leave to soak for 30 minutes.
2   Meanwhile, slice 250 g (8 oz) of the onions and finely chop the remainder. Cut the beef into large cubes.
3   Put the garlic and ginger in a mortar and use the pestle to pound together to form a smooth paste. Alternatively, use the side of a wide-bladed knife to pound them together.
4   Heat 60 ml (2 fl oz) oil in a heavy-based saucepan or flameproof casserole over a medium heat and fry the sliced onions for about 10 minutes, stirring occasionally, until dark brown and crisp. Use a slotted spoon to transfer the onions to kitchen paper.
5   In the same oil over a high heat, stir-fry the black cumin seeds, garlic and ginger paste and chopped onions until the onions are tender.
6   Add the beef and continue stir-frying until all the pieces look opaque and slightly fried. Cover the pan, lower the heat and simmer for about 5 minutes.
7   Stir in 250 ml (8 fl oz) water, the yogurt, salt, garam masala and bay leaf, then cover the pan again and bring to the boil. Lower the heat and simmer for about 45 minutes until all the liquid is absorbed and the meat is tender. If all the liquid is absorbed before the meat is tender, stir in a little more water and continue simmering. If the meat is tender before all liquid is absorbed, remove the meat pieces and cook the mixture, uncovered, over a high heat, stirring occasionally.
8   Remove from the heat and stir in the cream, crisp onions and chopped fresh coriander. Set aside.
9   Meanwhile, while the beef mixture is simmering, drain the rice. Heat the oil in another heavy-based pan or flameproof

continued on page 50

Beef Biryani continued from page 48

Cook's Tip
Look in Asian food shops for vetiver water, an intensely-flavoured flower water used in exotic cooking in India. If you find any, add ½ teaspoon to the saffron milk.

casserole over a high heat and add the black cumin seeds, cardamom pods, cloves and cinnamon.

10 When the seeds splutter, add the drained rice, stirring to coat each grain in oil. Stir in 750 ml (24 fl oz) water and bring to the boil. Cover the pan, lower the heat and simmer for about 8 minutes until the liquid is absorbed and grains are almost tender.

11 Meanwhile, soak the saffron threads in the warm milk. About 30 minutes before you want to serve, set the oven to 150C, 300F, Gas 2.

12 Put half the beef mixture in the washed-out casserole or an ovenproof dish with a tight-fitting lid. Top with half the rice, then layer with the remaining beef mixture and rice. Spoon the saffron and milk over the top. Cover and bake for 30 minutes.

CUCUMBER SALAD
Cachoomber

Time to make: 5 minutes
Serves 4 to 6

250 g (8 oz) cucumbers
250 g (8 oz) onions
250 g (8 oz) tomatoes
1 fresh green chilli
2 tablespoons chopped coriander
2 tablespoons lemon juice
2 teaspoons salt
½ teaspoon ground pepper

A refreshing combination of cucumber, tomatoes and onions, which is almost a must with a biryani.

1 Begin by preparing all the vegetables. Finely chop the cucumbers and onions, then seed and finely chop the tomatoes and green chillies.

2 Combine all the ingredients in a bowl, stirring until well blended together. Cover and refrigerate until ready to serve. Transfer to a serving bowl.

POTATOES AND YOGURT

Aloo Raita

Time to make: 10 minutes, plus
 cooling
Time to cook: 10 to 15 minutes
Serves 4 to 6

500 g (1 lb) potatoes

2 teaspoons cumin seeds

440 g (14 oz) plain yogurt

2 teaspoons salt

¼ teaspoon ground black pepper

2 tablespoons chopped fresh coriander

¼ teaspoon chilli powder

Even though this the simplest and most commonly made raita, I still think it is delicious. I like all raitas served very cold, so I make this up at least an hour before I plan to serve it.

1 Put the potatoes in a large saucepan of water and bring the water to the boil, then continue boiling for 10 to 15 minutes until the potatoes are tender. Drain well and set aside to cool.
2 When the potatoes are cool enough to handle, peel them and cut into small cubes.
3 Meanwhile, roast the cumin seeds in a heavy-based saucepan over a medium heat, stirring constantly, until dark brown. Pour the seeds out of the pan and leave until cool. When the cumin seeds are cool, grind them to a fine powder.
4 Put the yogurt in a bowl and beat until it is smooth, adding a little water to make a thick pouring consistency.
5 Stir in the salt, 1 teaspoon of the ground cumin seeds, the black pepper and 1 tablespoon of the coriander leaves.
6 Stir in the potatoes and stir until everything is evenly blended. Transfer to a serving dish and garnish with the remaining cumin seeds and coriander and the chilli powder. Serve immediately or chill until required.

SPICED MINCED BEEF

Keema

Time to make: 5 minutes
Time to cook: 20 to 25 minutes
Serves 4 to 6

---

250 g (8 oz) onions

250 g (8 oz) tomatoes

125 ml (4 fl oz) vegetable oil

2 teaspoons cumin seeds

1 tablespoon chopped garlic

1 tablespoon chopped peeled fresh root ginger

2 bay leaves

1 teaspoon garam masala, see page 9

1 tablespoon salt

1 tablespoon ground coriander

½ teaspoon turmeric

½ teaspoon chilli powder

½ teaspoon ground pepper

500 g (1 lb) lean minced beef

chopped fresh coriander leaves, to garnish

A very versatile dish that can easily be stretched to feed a larger number of people by adding peas and cooked potatoes just before it finishes cooking so they heat through. In my family, the decision to add peas or not depends on if my daughter is visiting because she doesn't like them.

1 Grate the onions and finely chop the tomatoes.
2 Heat the oil in a heavy-based saucepan over a high heat, then add the cumin seeds.
3 When the seeds splutter, stir in the garlic, ginger, onions, bay leaves and garam masala and stir-fry until the fat separates.
4 Add the tomatoes and continue stir-frying until the fat separates again, then stir in the salt, ground coriander, turmeric, chilli powder and black pepper. Stir in the meat and continue stir-frying, using a spoon to break up the meat, until it changes colour and loses any redness.
5 Lower the heat and continue stir-frying for about 15 minutes until the meat is cooked through and the fat separates again. Transfer to a serving dish and garnish with chopped coriander. Serve immediately.

Menu 10: Spiced Minced Beef, above, served with Cumin-spiced Squash, see page 55, and Five Pulses Cooked Together, see page 54.

FIVE PULSES COOKED TOGETHER

Pachmela Dahl

Time to make: 15 minutes
Time to cook: about 1 hour
Serves 4 to 6

3 tablespoons split yellow mung beans

3 tablespoons split green gram

3 tablespoons yellow lentils

3 tablespoons split and husked black gram

3 tablespoons split and husked Bengal gram

2 teaspoons salt

½ teaspoon turmeric

60 g (2 oz) onion

2 tablespoons vegetable oil, or 30 g (1 oz) ghee, see page 18

1 teaspoon cumin seeds

large pinch ground asafoetida

½ teaspoon chopped garlic

½ teaspoon chopped peeled fresh root ginger

1 teaspoon ground coriander

½ teaspoon chilli powder

½ teaspoon ground dried mango

chopped fresh coriander and sprigs, to garnish

A popular dish from Rajasthan, where it is part of a traditional menu and served with fried dumplings called *baati*.

1   Put the yellow mung beans, green gram, yellow lentils, black gram and Bengal gram in a large heavy-based saucepan and add 900 ml (32 fl oz) water, the salt and turmeric and place over a high heat.

2   Partially cover the pan and bring the water to the boil, then lower the heat and simmer, stirring occasionally, until the pulses are the consistency you prefer. This is a matter of personal taste.

3   Meanwhile, grate the onion.

4   When the pulses are cooked, heat the oil or melt the ghee in another heavy-based saucepan or wok over a high heat, then add the cumin seeds and ground asafoetida.

5   When the seeds splutter, add the onion, garlic and ginger and stir-fry until the onion turns brown and the fat separates. Stir in the ground coriander, chilli powder and ground dried mango.

6   Stir in the cooked pulses, stirring until well blended together. Bring to the boil, then simmer, uncovered, for 5 to 10 minutes until well mixed and the flavours are blended. Transfer to a serving dish and garnish with the chopped fresh coriander and sprigs. Serve immediately.

CUMIN-SPICED SQUASH
Ghiya Malaiwala

Time to make: 5 minutes
Time to cook: 20 to 25 minutes
Serves 4 to 6

---

500 g (1 lb) squash, such as acorn squash or courgettes

2 tablespoons vegetable oil

2 teaspoons cumin seeds

2 teaspoons salt

60 ml (2 fl oz) double cream

1 fresh green chilli, finely chopped, to garnish

In India, I can make this with a long, slender squash called bottle gourd. You might be lucky and find this at an Indian greengrocer, but most of the time you will have to substitute another squash. Just take care that, whatever squash you use, it is not overcooked and too soft.

1   Peel the squash, then cut it into slices about 2 cm (¾ in) thick.
2   Heat the oil in a heavy-based saucepan over a high heat and add the cumin seeds.
3   When the seeds splutter, add the squash and salt and stir a few times until the squash slices look glossy.
4   Cover the pan, lower the heat and simmer for about 20 minutes until the slices of squash are just tender. The exact time will depend on freshness of squash.
5   Uncover, stir in the cream and continue cooking over a medium heat until the mixture looks creamy and is no longer runny. Transfer to a serving dish and garnish with chopped green chilli. Serve immediately.

CURRIED MEATBALLS

Keema Ke Kofte

Time to make: 20 minutes, plus chilling
Time to cook: 45 minutes
Makes about 15

1½ teaspoons chopped garlic
1½ teaspoons chopped ginger
500 g (1 lb) lean minced beef or lamb
1 teaspoon salt
¼ teaspoon ground black pepper
¼ teaspoon garam masala

For the curried gravy

500 g (1 lb) onions
500 g (1 lb) tomatoes
1 tablespoon chopped garlic
1 tablespoon chopped peeled fresh root ginger
60 ml (2 fl oz) vegetable oil
1 tablespoon cumin seeds
2 or 3 bay leaves
2 tablespoons ground coriander
2 teaspoons garam masala
1 tablespoon salt
½ teaspoon chilli powder
½ teaspoon turmeric
2 tablespoons single cream, to garnish
chopped fresh coriander leaves, to garnish

Menu 11: Curried Meatballs, above, served with Spiced Rice, see page 59, and Five Vegetables Cooked Together, see page 58.

Once I would have fried the meatballs before adding them to this spicy gravy but my parents' cook, Sailor, showed me how to add them raw. I think this tastes better, and it cuts down on the amount of fat in the dish.

1 To make the meatballs, put the garlic and ginger in a mortar and use the pestle to pound them together to form a smooth paste. Alternatively, use the side of a wide-bladed knife to pound them together.

2 Put the garlic and ginger paste in a bowl with the minced beef or lamb, salt, black pepper and garam masala and mix everything together until well blended.

3 Lightly wet your hands and shape the mixture into about 15 meatballs, each the size of a walnut. Put the meatballs on a plate, cover with plastic wrap and refrigerate for at least 1 hour.

4 Meanwhile, to make curried gravy, roughly chop the onions and finely chop the tomatoes.

5 Put the garlic, ginger and onions in a blender or food processor and process until a smooth paste forms.

6 Heat the oil in a heavy-based saucepan or wok over a high heat, then add the cumin seeds and bay leaves. When the seeds splutter, stir in the onion mixture and stir until it turns light brown.

7 Stir in the tomatoes, ground coriander, garam masala, salt, chilli powder and turmeric, stirring until well blended together. Lower the heat and continue cooking, stirring occasionally, for about 8 minutes until the fat separates.

8 Stir in 625 ml (20 fl oz) water, then increase the heat and bring to the boil. Add the meatballs and bring the mixture to the boil again, then lower the heat and simmer for about 20 minutes until the meatballs are cooked through. The meatballs will shrink by at least one-quarter while they cook, and will not be pink in the centre if you cut one in half. Transfer them to a serving dish, spoon over the cream and garnish with chopped coriander. Serve immediately.

FIVE VEGETABLES COOKED TOGETHER

Pachrangi Sabzi

Time to make: 10 to 15 minutes
Time to cook: 25 to 35 minutes
Serves 4 to 6

---

250 g (8 oz) potatoes

250 g (8 oz) cauliflower

125 g (4 oz) sweet red pepper

125 g (4 oz) carrots

125 g (4 oz) aubergine

125 ml (4 fl oz) vegetable oil

1 teaspoon cumin seeds

large pinch ground asafoetida

1 tablespoon finely chopped peeled fresh root ginger

4 teaspoons ground coriander

1 teaspoon chilli powder

1 teaspoon fennel seeds

½ teaspoon turmeric

½ teaspoon garam masala, see page 9

2 teaspoons ground dried mango

125 g (4 oz) plain yogurt, beaten until smooth

I have fond memories of when my daughter was young because she would come into the kitchen and mix and match the vegetables for this dish. This is a combination of vegetables I particularly enjoy, but you can, of course, vary the selection with the season. Just make sure vegetables are cut to a size and thickness so they cook in same amount of time. The potatoes and cauliflower, for example, should be slightly smaller because they take longer to cook.

1 To prepare the vegetables (see introduction), chop the potatoes and break the cauliflower into florets. Core, seed and slice the pepper into long strips. Peel and slice the carrot lengthways and slice the aubergine lengthways.

2 Heat the oil in a heavy-based saucepan over a high heat, then add the cumin seeds and ground asafoetida.

3 When the seeds splutter, add the ginger and stir-fry until light brown. Add the potatoes, cauliflower, red pepper, carrot and aubergine and continue stir-frying until they are glossy.

4 Stir in the ground coriander, chilli powder, fennel seeds, turmeric and garam masala. Cover the pan, lower the heat and simmer, stirring occasionally so the vegetables don't scorch, for 20 to 30 minutes until they are tender.

5 Uncover the pan and stir in the ground dried mango and yogurt, then stir-fry over a medium heat until the moisture evaporates. Transfer to a serving dish. Serve immediately.

SPICED RICE

Vagharela Chawal

Time to make: 10 minutes, plus
    soaking
Time to cook: about 30 minutes
Serves 4 to 6

---

250 g (8 oz) long-grain rice, preferably basmati

375 g (12 oz) onions

60 ml (2 fl oz) vegetable oil

1 tablespoon sugar

1 black cardamom pod

large pinch of freshly crushed cinnamon stick or ground

1 teaspoon salt

This is a Parsi preparation, made specifically to accompany *dhansak*, a lentil dish, but I like this aromatic dish so much because of its rich flavour that I often prepare it to accompany other lentil dishes and meat curries. I was first introduced to this spiced rice by my Parsi friends.

1 Put the rice in a fine sieve and rinse under running cold water until the water runs clear.

2 Put the rice and enough water to cover in a bowl and leave the rice to soak for 30 minutes.

3 Meanwhile, thinly slice 250 g (8 oz) of the onions and grate the remainder.

4 Heat the oil in a heavy-based saucepan over a high heat. Add the sliced onions, then lower the heat and cook, stirring occasionally, for about 10 minutes until the onions are dark brown and crisp.

5 Use a slotted spoon to remove the onions from the oil and drain them well on kitchen paper.

6 Add the sugar to the hot oil in the saucepan over a medium heat and cook for about 2 minutes until the sugar caramelises and turns dark brown.

7 Stir in the grated onions, cardamom pod and cinnamon and continue cooking, stirring occasionally, for 2 to 3 minutes until the onions turn light brown.

8 Drain the rice. Add the rice to the pan with the salt, stirring to coat all the grains, then add 625 ml (20 fl oz) water and bring to the boil, uncovered.

9 When the water boils, cover the pan, lower the heat to low and simmer for about 10 minutes until all the water is absorbed and the grains are tender. Transfer to a serving dish and garnish with the crispy, fried onions. Serve immediately.

BEEF CURRY

Gosht Rasedar

Time to make: 15 minutes
Time to cook: about 1½ hours
Serves 4 to 6

500 g (1 lb) lean beef, such as shoulder or leg
500 g (1 lb) tomatoes
2 tablespoons single cream, to garnish
2 tablespoons chopped fresh coriander leaves, to garnish

For the masala

500 g (1 lb) onions
1 tablespoon peeled chopped fresh root ginger
1 tablespoon chopped garlic
60 ml (2 fl oz) vegetable oil
1 tablespoon cumin seeds
2 or 3 bay leaves
1 tablespoon salt
1 tablespoon ground coriander
2 teaspoons garam masala, see page 9
½ teaspoon chilli powder
½ teaspoon turmeric

It's a misconception that all curries taste the same. In fact, there are many different flavour combinations. After you have followed this recipe once or twice, you can vary it in so many different ways. Some cooks I know like to substitute yogurt for the tomatoes, while others leave the onions out all together.

1   Begin by making the masala. Roughly chop the onions. Put the onions, ginger and garlic in a blender or food processor and process until a smooth paste forms.
2   Cut the beef into large cubes and finely chop the tomatoes.
3   Heat the oil for the masala in a heavy-based saucepan or flameproof casserole over a high heat and add the cumin seeds and bay leaves.
4   When the seeds splutter, stir in the onion paste and stir-fry until light brown. Add the salt, ground coriander, garam masala, chilli powder and turmeric and stir 4 or 5 times until well blended together.
5   Add the beef cubes to the masala and stir until they become opaque, which means the juices have been sealed in. Cover the pan, lower the heat and simmer for about 30 minutes, stirring occasionally, until all the liquid is absorbed and the mixture begins to stick to the pan.
6   Stir in the finely chopped tomatoes and continue simmering, covered, for 30 to 35 minutes until the tomatoes are cooked and the fat separates.
7   Stir in 625 ml (1 pint) water, then turn up the heat and return to the boil. Cover the pan, lower the heat and simmer again for about 20 minutes until the meat is cooked through and tender. Transfer to a serving dish, stir in the cream and garnish with chopped coriander. Serve immediately.

Menu 12: Beef Curry, above, served with Sautéed Peas and Chapatis, both on page 62.

SAUTÉED PEAS

Chhonke Hue Mattar

Time to make: 5 minutes
Time to cook: about 12 minutes
Serves 4 to 6

---

1 kg (2 lb) fresh peas, or 375 g (12 oz) frozen peas, thawed

60 ml (2 fl oz) vegetable oil

2 teaspoons cumin seeds

large pinch ground asafoetida

1 tablespoon finely sliced peeled fresh root ginger

1 tablespoon ground coriander

2 teaspoons salt

1 tablespoon lemon juice

1 tablespoon chopped fresh coriander leaves

finely shredded lemon rind, to garnish

It wasn't until after I moved to Delhi that I started making this dish, because in Bombay, where I grew up, the peas are not as good. It's a popular winter dish in my household and I have to admit that by spring I'm quite happy not to eat peas again for some time.

1   If you are using fresh peas, shell them.
2   Heat the oil in a heavy-based saucepan over a high heat, then add the cumin seeds and ground asafoetida. When the seeds splutter, add the ginger and stir-fry until it turns light brown.
3   Stir in the peas, ground coriander and salt and continue stir-frying until peas look glossy. Partially cover the pan, lower the heat and simmer for about 10 minutes until the peas are just tender. The exact time will depend on the quality of peas; any tough peas may need a little water added.
4   Stir in the lemon juice and chopped coriander. Transfer to a serving dish and garnish with lemon rind. Serve immediately.

CHAPATIS

This wholemeal flat bread is part of the staple diet for many Indians. Rolling out the dough can take a bit of practice. Do not press the rolling pin too firmly over the dough. Instead, just hold it lightly and let it roll to and fro in your hands. Hold your left hand steady and push the dough clockwise with your right hand, so it keeps an even, round shape, lightly rolling in between each turn. Try to make the dough as thin as you can without it tearing and add as much extra flour as necessary to prevent the dough sticking. These freeze well, so it is worth making a batch when you have the time.

Place 315 g (10 oz) plain wholemeal flour in a deep bowl and make a well in centre. Pour in about 125 ml (4 fl oz) water and gradually mix together, slowly adding about an additional 125 ml (4 fl oz) water to form a slightly sticky dough. Roll dough around the bowl to pick up all flour, then knead until soft and smooth. You should be able to press your finger into the dough with hardly any pressure. Flatten dough and make impressions in it with your fingertips. Sprinkle water over and leave dough 30 minutes.

Knead dough a little, then form it into a long roll. Break off about 12 walnut-sized pieces. Roll into smooth balls, then flatten each.

On a well-floured surface, roll the flattened dough into thin 13 cm (5 in) rounds (see the introduction). As you roll out each piece, keep it covered with a towel, then continue until all the pieces are rolled out.

Heat the griddle or *tawa* over a high heat until if a drop of water is thrown over, it will evaporate immediately with a sizzling sound. Cook one chapati at a time until the edges start rising and bubbles form on the surface. Lift it with a pair of tongs (the experts use their fingers!) and place it over a gas flame, uncooked side down; it should start puffing up immediately. When it is puffed up, or a spotty brown on the underside, flip it over to cook other side a bit more. Remove from the flame and brush with melted ghee, if you like, or serve plain. Serve immediately.

DEEP-FRIED MARINATED FISH

Tali Hui Machhi

Time to make: 10 minutes, plus
chilling
Time to cook: 10 to 15 minutes
Serves 4 to 6

**500 g (1 lb) meaty white fish,
such as cod or haddock, cut
from the middle section**

75 g (2½ oz) onion

2 teaspoons chopped garlic

**2 teaspoons chopped peeled
fresh root ginger**

**60 g (2 oz) plain yogurt or
1 tablespoon malt vinegar**

1 teaspoon chilli powder

½ teaspoon turmeric

1 teaspoon salt

**¼ teaspoon garam masala, see
page 9**

vegetable oil for deep-frying

**chopped fresh coriander and
lemon wedges, to garnish**

Here's a popular road-side dish throughout northern India, especially during the winter. Not skinned, this fish is simply deep-fried without a batter. If you don't have any coriander chutney made up, this also tastes good with just a squeeze of lemon juice over each piece. You can also pan-fry the fish, but I prefer it cooked this way because the skin is nice and crisp.

1 Cut the fish into 1 cm (½ in) thick slices, and roughly chop the onion.
2 Put the onion, garlic and ginger in a blender or food processor and process until a smooth paste forms.
3 Put the onion paste, yogurt or vinegar, chilli powder, turmeric, salt and garam masala in a bowl and stir together until well blended. Add the fish, stirring gently to coat all the pieces in the marinade. Cover the bowl and refrigerate for 1 to 2 hours, or longer if possible.
4 When ready to fry the fish, use a slotted spoon to remove the pieces from the marinade and place them on a wire rack set over a baking sheet for an hour or so. This is important because if the fish isn't well drained the excess liquid with splash a lot and bubble up in the hot oil and it will be difficult to handle.
5 Heat the oil in a large, heavy-based saucepan or wok over a high heat. When the oil is hot enough that a piece of bread will immediately return to the surface when it is dropped in, add as many fish pieces as will fit. Do not over-crowd the pan. Lower the heat to medium and fry the fish, stirring occasionally with a long-handled spoon, until they are golden brown.
6 Use a slotted spoon to remove the fish pieces from the hot oil and place on kitchen towels to drain. Keep warm while frying the remaining fish. Transfer to a serving plate and garnish with coriander and lemon wedges for squeezing over each portion. Serve immediately.

BENGALI-SPICED POTATOES

Aloor Dum

Time to make: 20 minutes
Time to cook: 20 minutes
Serves 4 to 6

---

500 g (1 lb) small potatoes

2 or 3 fresh green chillies

2 teaspoons chopped peeled
fresh root ginger

125 g (4 oz) plain yogurt

1 tablespoon salt

2 teaspoons ground coriander

½ teaspoon turmeric

¼ teaspoon ground black
pepper

30 g (1 oz) ghee, see page 18

7 to 8 fresh curry leaves or
½ teaspoon dried and crushed

1 teaspoon cumin seeds

2 teaspoons sugar

large pinch ground cloves

large pinch ground cinnamon

large pinch ground cardamom

fresh mint sprigs, to garnish

I never tire of potatoes and I'm always on the lookout for new recipes. I particularly recommend these potatoes eaten with a paratha, see page 27.

1 Try to select potatoes small enough to be boiled whole. If not, cut large potatoes into 4 cm (1½ in) cubes. Put the potatoes in a large pan of water and bring to the boil, then continue to boil for 10 to 15 minutes until they are tender. Drain well. When cool enough to handle, peel the potatoes and chop.

2 Meanwhile, seed and roughly chop the green chillies.

3 Put the green chillies and ginger in a mortar and use the pestle to pound together to form a smooth paste. Alternatively, use the side of a wide-bladed knife to pound them together.

4 Put the chilli paste, potatoes, yogurt, salt, ground coriander, turmeric and black pepper in a bowl and stir together until well blended.

5 Melt the ghee in a heavy-based saucepan over a high heat, then add the curry leaves and cumin seeds.

6 When the seeds splutter, add the potato mixture and cook, stirring occasionally, for 4 to 6 minutes until the fat separates.

7 Turn off the heat. Stir together the sugar, ground cloves, ground cinnamon and ground cardamom in a bowl, then stir the mixture into the potato mixture. Transfer to a serving dish and garnish with mint sprigs. Serve immediately.

Note
If you don't want to serve this dish immediately, remove from heat after step 6 and set aside. Just before serving, re-heat and stir in the sugar and ground spices.

Menu 13: Deep-fried Marinated Fish, see page 63, served with Bengali-spiced Potatoes, above, and Coconut and Coriander Chutney, see page 72.

MONKFISH OR COD TIKKA

Macchli Ke Tikke

Time to make: 10 minutes, plus
marinating and chilling
Time to cook: 20 minutes
Serves 4 to 6

---

500 g (1 lb) monkfish or cod fillet

---

salt

---

1 tablespoon lemon juice

---

2 tablespoons chopped garlic

---

2 tablespoons chopped peeled fresh root ginger

---

220 g (7 oz) plain yogurt, or 3 tablespoons malt vinegar

---

2 teaspoons chilli powder

---

1 teaspoon ground black pepper

---

1 teaspoon chaat ka masala, see page 9

---

few drops red food colouring, optional

---

1 lime, cut into wedges, to garnish

---

1 onion, thinly sliced into rings, to garnish

---

chopped fresh mint leaves, to garnish

Cook's Tip
When you are in a real hurry, use a tandoori masala from the supermarket or some Dry Tandoori Masala, see page 11.

Menu 14: Monkfish Tikka, above, served on Rice with Lentils and topped with Tomato-Mint Raita, both on page 68.

Traditionally, these pieces of fish are skewered and cooked in a *tandoor*, like tandoori chicken, but most home cooks today use the grill or the barbecue. Made without any added fat, this dish is not only tasty, but also good for weight-watchers. For cocktail parties, I serve cubes of cooked fish on a platter sprinkled with thinly sliced onion rings, lemon juice and salt.

1   Skin the fish fillet, then cut the flesh into 4 cm (1½ in) cubes. Put the monkfish or cod cubes in a glass bowl with 1 teaspoon salt and the lemon juice and stir gently until all the cubes are coated, then leave to marinate for 15 minutes.
2   Put the fish in a fine nylon sieve or colander and rinse well with running cold water, then leave to drain well.
3   Put the garlic and ginger in a mortar and use the pestle to pound together to form a smooth paste. Alternatively, use the side of a wide-bladed knife to pound them together.
4   Put the garlic and ginger paste, drained fish, yogurt or vinegar, chilli powder, black pepper, chaat ka masala, 1 tablespoon salt and red food colouring, if desired, in a glass bowl and gently stir together until all the fish cubes are coated with the marinade. Cover and refrigerate for at least 2 hours, gently stirring occasionally.
5   Set the oven to 200C, 400F, Gas 6. Use a slotted spoon to remove the fish cubes from the marinade and place them on a wire rack set over a baking sheet. Bake for about 20 minutes or until the flesh flakes easily if tested with the tip of a knife. Transfer to a serving plate and garnish with lemon wedges for squeezing over each portion, onion rings and chopped mint.

RICE WITH LENTILS
Khilee Hui Khichdee

Time to make: 5 minutes, plus
  soaking
Time to cook: 15 minutes
Serves 4 to 6

---

250 g (8 oz) basmati rice

**100 g (3½ oz) split and husked
yellow lentils**

2 tablespoons ghee, see page 9

1 teaspoon cumin seeds

pinch of ground asafoetida

1 teaspoon ground coriander

2 teaspoons salt

I simply love this dish made with all kinds of lentils. I am very satisfied when I can eat this dish with a bowl of yogurt and Mango Pickle, see page 13.

1   Put the rice and lentils in a fine sieve and rinse under running cold water until the water runs clear, then place in a bowl with enough water to cover to soak for at least 30 minutes.
2   Drain the rice and lentils. Melt the ghee in a heavy-based saucepan over a high heat, then add the cumin seeds and asafoetida. When the seeds splutter, add the rice and lentil mixture, ground coriander and salt, stirring to coat all the grains and lentils in oil. Stir-fry for 2 minutes until the water evaporates.
3   Stir in 625 ml (20 fl oz) water and bring to the boil. Cover the pan, lower the heat to low and simmer for 10 minutes until all the water is absorbed and the rice and lentils are tender. Transfer to a serving dish and serve.

TOMATO-MINT RAITA
Tamattar-Poodine Ka Raita

Time to make: 10 minutes
Serves 4 to 6

---

2 teaspoons cumin seeds

315 g (10 oz) tomatoes

60 g (2 oz) fresh mint leaves

440 g (14 oz) plain yogurt

2 teaspoons salt

¼ teaspoon black pepper

**¼ teaspoon chilli powder, to
garnish**

This refreshing accompaniment is ready to serve as soon as it is mixed together, but I prefer to chill it for at least one hour.

1   Roast the cumin seeds in a heavy-based saucepan over a medium heat, stirring constantly, until dark brown. Immediately pour out of the pan and leave to cool. Grind to a fine powder.
2   Seed and finely chop the tomatoes. Finely chop the mint leaves. Put the yogurt in a bowl and beat until smooth, adding a little water to make a thick pouring consistency. Stir in the salt, 1 teaspoon ground cumin seeds and the pepper.
3   Stir in the tomatoes and mint. Garnish with the remaining cumin seeds and chilli powder. Chill or serve immediately.

DELICATELY SPICED YOGURT CURRY

Gujerati Kadhi

Time to make: 10 minutes
Time to cook: about 20 minutes
Serves 4 to 6

---

440 g (14 oz) plain yogurt

¼ teaspoon citric acid

2 tablespoons chick-pea flour

2 to 3 tablespoons sugar, to taste

1 tablespoon salt

1 teaspoon chilli powder

¼ teaspoon ground asafoetida

¼ teaspoon ground cinnamon

2 tablespoons vegetable oil

2 teaspoons mustard seeds

8 to 10 fresh curry leaves or 1 teaspoon dried and crushed

3 or 4 whole dried red chillies

chopped fresh coriander leaves, to garnish

Typical of food from the Gujerat region, this is a thin curry made with yogurt. It is so thin, in fact, that I sometimes like to drink it like a soup.

1 Put the yogurt and citric acid in a large bowl and beat until it is smooth. Add the chick-pea flour and stir until they are well blended together. Sir in the sugar, salt, chilli powder, ground asafoetida, ground cinnamon and 900 ml (32 fl oz) water.
2 Heat the oil in a heavy-based saucepan over a high heat, then add the mustard seeds, curry leaves and dried red chillies.
3 When the seeds splutter, stir in the yogurt mixture and bring to the boil. Lower the heat and simmer, uncovered for 15 to 20 minutes until the yogurt is about the consistency of whole milk. Transfer to a serving bowl and garnish with chopped coriander. Serve immediately.

STEAMED CHICK-PEA PATTIES
Muthia

Time to make: about 10 minutes, plus resting
Time to cook: 15 to 20 minutes
Makes 12 to 15

---

220 g (7 oz) fresh fenugreek leaves

---

125 g (4 oz) chick-pea flour

---

45 g (1½ oz) plain wholemeal flour

1½ teaspoons salt

½ teaspoon chilli powder

½ teaspoon turmeric

---

2 tablespoons vegetable oil

On a rainy day in India, we love to eat something piping hot, preferably fried, with our cup of tea. This is one of the recipes I enjoy the most. On such a day, I like to fry the patties and add some chopped green chillies and coriander leaves to make them even spicier.

1 Finely chop the fenugreek leaves.
2 Put the fenugreek leaves, chick-pea flour, wholemeal flour, salt, chilli powder and turmeric in a bowl and stir until thoroughly combined. Stir in oil and mix together to form a dough. Lightly knead dough in a bowl until it is soft and smooth. Shape dough into a ball and place back in bowl. Cover the bowl and leave the dough to rest for at least 15 minutes.
3 Divide the dough into 12 to 15 walnut-size pieces and roll into smooth balls. Lightly press the balls between your palms to flatten.
4 To steam, place the patties in a steamer over boiling water, cover and steam for 15 to 20 minutes until a skewer inserted in the centre comes out clean. Steam in batches if necessary. Transfer to a serving platter. Serve immediately.

Cook's Tip
If fresh fenugreek leaves are unavailable, substitute dried fenugreek leaves along with 1 teaspoon ground fenugreek. If you do use the dried leaves, however, you will have to add a little water when you knead the dough because it is the fresh leaves that provide the necessary moisture.

Variation
I like to serve fried chick-pea patties with chutney as a snack or accompaniment to cocktails. To fry the patties, heat enough oil to cover them in a heavy-based saucepan over a high heat. Add a few patties at a time, then lower the heat and fry for 6 to 7 minutes on both sides until if you cut through one, it is cooked all the way through but still soft in the centre.

Menu 15: Delicately Spiced Yogurt Curry, see page 69, served with Steamed Chick-pea Patties, above, and Lemon Rice, see page 26.

COCONUT AND CORIANDER CHUTNEY

Hari, Nariyal Ki Chutney

Time to make: 15 to 20 minutes
Makes about 350 g (12 oz)

---

125 g (4 oz) fresh coconut or 45 g (1½ oz) desiccated

125 g (4 oz) fresh coriander leaves

125 g (4 oz) onion

30 g (1 oz) fresh green chillies

1 teaspoon chopped garlic

1 teaspoon chopped ginger

2.5 cm (1 in) ball of tamarind or ½ teaspoon tamarind concentrate

4 teaspoons salt

1 tablespoon sugar

2 tablespoons lime juice

At least six times a year when someone comes to visit from Bombay, they bring small polythene bags of this delicious chutney from my parents' cook, Angela. This has always been a family favourite, and Angela, now in her seventies, is very proud that no one makes it quite as good as she does. Still, I think you will enjoy my version, which is, of course, based on Angela's!

Originally from the coastal regions, this recipe is good served as a relish with various snacks. It also makes an interesting sandwich filling.

1   Peel the fresh coconut so you end up with 100 g (3½ oz) coconut flesh. Grate the coconut flesh into a blender or food processor. If you are using desiccated coconut, soak it in water to cover for 30 minutes, then strain it.

2   Roughly chop the coriander leaves, onions and green chillies.

3   Put all the ingredients in a blender or food processor and process until a fine paste forms. Add a little water only if the chutney is too stiff. Keep in a covered container in the fridge for about 1 week.

Cook's Tip

For a quick supper, coat pieces of fish or shrimp with this chutney, then wrap them tightly in foil and steam them until the fish flakes easily and the shrimp turn pink.

PEAS AND PANEER

Mattar Paneer Rasedar

Time to make: 10 to 15 minutes
Time to cook: 25 to 35 minutes
Serves 4 to 6

---

500 g (1 lb) paneer, see page 19

vegetable oil for deep frying paneer

---

125 g (4 oz) tomatoes

---

1 kg (2 lb) fresh peas or 375 g (12 oz) frozen peas, thawed

---

250 g (8 oz) onions

---

2 or 4 fresh green chillies

---

1 teaspoon chopped garlic

---

1 teaspoon chopped peeled fresh root ginger

---

60 ml (2 fl oz) vegetable oil

---

2 teaspoons cumin seeds

---

2 bay leaves

---

1 tablespoon salt

---

1 tablespoon ground coriander

½ teaspoon turmeric

½ teaspoon garam masala, see page 9

½ teaspoon chilli powder

---

chopped fresh coriander leaves, to garnish

For this version of this gravied dish you will be familiar with from your local Indian restaurant, I suggest that you lightly fry the cubes of paneer before you add them to the other ingredients.

1   Begin by preparing the paneer. Cut the paneer into cubes. Heat the oil in a heavy-based saucepan or wok over a high heat. Add the paneer cubes and deep-fry, stirring occasionally, until light brown on all sides. Remove from the oil with a slotted spoon and drain well on kitchen paper. Turn off the heat off.
2   Finely chop the tomatoes. If you are using fresh peas, shell them. Roughly chop the onions and make a slit in each of the green chillies.
3   Put the onions, garlic and ginger in a blender or food processor and process until a smooth paste forms.
4   Heat 60 ml (2 fl oz) oil in the heavy-based saucepan or wok over a high heat, then add the cumin seeds and bay leaves.
5   When the seeds splutter, stir in the onion paste and stir-fry for about 5 minutes until light brown and the fat separates.
6   Add the tomatoes, salt, ground coriander, turmeric, garam masala and chilli powder and continue stir-frying for 8 to 10 minutes until the fat separates again.
7   Stir in the peas, paneer and green chillies and continue stir-frying until the peas look glossy. Stir in 500 ml (16 fl oz) water and bring to the boil, then cover the pan, lower the heat and simmer for 10 to 15 minutes. Transfer to a serving dish and garnish with chopped coriander. Serve immediately.

Cook's Tip
If you want to save time, fry the cubes two or three days ahead and keep them refrigerated until you need them. In fact, I find paneer freezes very well if it has been lightly fried, but if you try to freeze it without frying it first, it will just crumble.

SAUTÉED AUBERGINE

Baingan Ka Bharta

Time to make: 15 to 20 minutes
Time to cook: 12 to 15 minutes
Serves 4 to 6

2 aubergines, each about 375 g (12 oz)
250 g (8 oz) onions
250 g (8 oz) tomatoes
3 or 4 fresh green chillies
60 ml (2 fl oz) vegetable oil
1 teaspoon cumin seeds
1 tablespoon finely chopped peeled fresh root ginger
1 tablespoon salt
1 tablespoon ground coriander
½ teaspoon turmeric
½ teaspoon chilli powder
½ teaspoon garam masala, see page 9
chopped fresh coriander leaves, to garnish

Bharta implies mashing, hence the name of this spicy aubergine dish with a slightly mashed texture. I like the onions and tomato to be bite-like but I know other cooks that prefer to finely chop them so they are less obvious.

1   Set the grill to high. Put the whole aubergines on the grill rack and grill, turning occasionally, until they are charred on all sides and the skins split.

2   Put the aubergines in a bowl of cold water and leave to cool. When they are cool enough to handle, peel them, then remove stems and finely chop. Set aside.

3   Meanwhile, coarsely chop the onions and chop the tomatoes the same size as the onions. Make a slit in each green chilli.

4   Heat the oil in a heavy-based saucepan or wok over a high heat, then add the cumin seeds.

5   When the seed splutter, add the onions and ginger and stir-fry until the onions look slightly fried.

6   Stir in the tomatoes and the chillies and continue stir-frying until the mixture looks glossy. Stir in the salt, ground coriander, turmeric, chilli powder and garam masala, stirring until well blended together.

7   Stir in the aubergines, then lower the heat and continue cooking, stirring often, for 8 to 10 minutes until the aubergines are cooked through and mixture is well blended. The onions and tomatoes should stay bite-like. Transfer to a serving dish and garnish with coriander. Serve immediately.

Menu 16: Peas and Paneer, see page 73, served with Sautéed Aubergine, above, and Cumin-flavoured Rice with Onions, see page 76.

CUMIN-FLAVOURED RICE WITH ONIONS

Jeere Ke Chawal

Time to make: 5 minutes, plus
  soaking
Time to cook: about 15 minutes
Serves 4 to 6

---

75 g (2½ oz) onion

250 g (8 oz) long-grain rice, preferable basmati

2 tablespoons vegetable oil

2 teaspoons cumin seeds

1 teaspoon salt

few drops of lemon juice

finely shredded lime rind, optional

As a child in Bombay, when my parents went out for the evening, we children could choose whatever we wanted for supper. We almost always chose this and Red Masala, see page 10.

Delicately flavoured with cumin, this rice is delicious served with dishes with lots of gravy, such as Goan-style Chicken Curry, see page 20, Beef Curry, see page 60, or Curried Meatballs, see page 56. It is also good with raita, see page 30.

1 Slice the onion.
2 Put the rice in a fine sieve and rinse under running cold water until the water runs clear.
3 Put the rice and enough water to cover in a bowl and leave the rice to soak for 30 minutes.
4 Heat the oil in a heavy-based saucepan over a high heat, then add the cumin seeds.
5 When the seeds splutter, add the onions and stir-fry for about 30 seconds until they are transparent but not browned.
6 Drain the rice. Add the rice and salt to the pan, stirring to coat all the grains in oil. Stir in 625 ml (20 fl oz) water and bring to the boil, uncovered.
7 When the water boils, add the lemon juice, then cover the pan, lower the heat to low and simmer for about 10 minutes until all the water is absorbed and the grains are tender. Transfer to a serving dish and garnish with lime rind, if desired. Serve immediately.

YELLOW LENTILS
Arhar Ki Dahl

Time to make: 5 minutes
Time to cook: about 55 minutes
Serves 4 to 6

185 g (6 oz) yellow lentils
1 tablespoon salt
1 teaspoon sugar
½ teaspoon turmeric
1 teaspoon ground dried mango
1 teaspoon ground coriander
½ teaspoon garam masala, see page 9
½ teaspoon chilli powder
2 tablespoons vegetable oil or 30 g (1 oz) ghee, see page 18
1 teaspoon cumin seeds
large pinch ground asafoetida
chopped fresh coriander leaves, to garnish

This is one of the most popular lentil dishes throughout India, but you'll find the use of different spices and the different consistency in each region makes it seem like a different dish wherever you go. This particular preparation is from the Uttar Pradesh region, or, as some say, made the way the *Delhiwalas* make it. It was several years after my marriage before my husband stopped saying 'this isn't like my mother's' every time I made this.

1 Rinse the lentils well, then drain them.
2 Put the lentils in a large, heavy-based saucepan. Add 900 ml (32 fl oz) water, the salt, sugar and turmeric and place over a high heat.
3 Partially cover the pan and bring the water to the boil, then lower the heat and simmer, stirring occasionally, for about 45 minutes until the lentils are soft.
4 Stir in the ground dried mango, ground coriander, garam masala and chilli powder, stirring until all the ingredients are well blended together.
5 To temper the lentils, heat the oil or melt the ghee in another heavy-based saucepan or wok over a high heat, then add the cumin seeds and ground asafoetida. When the seeds splutter, stir in the lentil mixture and bring to the boil, then lower the heat and simmer for about 1 minute, stirring until well blended together. Transfer to a serving dish and garnish with chopped coriander. Serve immediately.

Variation
Some people like to add the melted ghee and chilli powder to the hot lentils and just stir them in a little. The choice is personal.

POTATOES IN MUSTARD OIL AND SPICES

Tel Ke Aloo

Time to make: 5 minutes
Time to cook: 10 to 12 minutes
Serves 4 to 6

500 g (1 lb) potatoes

125 ml (4 fl oz) mustard oil

2 teaspoons cumin seeds

¼ teaspoon ground asafoetida

1 tablespoon ground coriander

1 tablespoon salt

2 teaspoons ground dried mango

1 teaspoon chilli powder

½ teaspoon turmeric

lime wedges and fresh mint, to garnish

Very small, bite-size new potatoes that can be cooked whole are ideal for this dish.

1   Scrub the potatoes well. If you don't have very small new potatoes, halve other new potatoes or cut large potatoes into 1 cm (½ in) dice.

2   Heat the oil in a heavy-based saucepan over a high heat, then add the cumin seeds and ground asafoetida.

3   When the seeds splutter, add the potatoes and cook, stirring occasionally, for about 2 minutes until the they change colour slightly and begin to look opaque, but not translucent.

4   Lower the heat and add the ground coriander, salt, ground dried mango, chilli powder and turmeric, stirring until well blended together.

5   Cover the pan, lower the heat and cook over a low heat, stirring occasionally so the potatoes don't scorch, for 8 to 10 minutes until they are tender and cooked through. Transfer to a serving dish and garnish with lime wedges and mint sprigs. Serve immediately.

Menu 17: Potatoes in Mustard Oil and Spices, above, and Yellow Lentils, see page 77, served with a Chapati, see page 62.

CURRY WITH FRIED DUMPLINGS

Besan Ki Kadhi

Time to make: 10 minutes
Time to cook: about 50 minutes
Serves 4 to 6

625 g (1¼ lb) plain yogurt
1 teaspoon vinegar or citric acid crystals
125 g (4 oz) chick-pea flour
2 tablespoons salt
2 teaspoons ground coriander
1 teaspoon chilli powder
1 teaspoon turmeric
¼ teaspoon ground asafoetida
60 ml (2 fl oz) vegetable oil
1 tablespoon coriander seeds
2 teaspoons fenugreek seeds
5 or 6 whole dried red chillies
7 to 8 fresh curry leaves or ½ teaspoon dried and crushed
chopped fresh coriander leaves, to garnish

For the dumplings

125 g (4 oz) chick-pea flour
1 teaspoon salt
¼ teaspoon bicarbonate of soda
vegetable oil for deep-frying

Menu 18: Curry with Fried Dumplings, above, served with Spicy Potatoes, see page 82, and Rice with Peas, see page 83.

A speciality of northern India, where you'll find the basic curry is pretty much the same in most homes, but the dumplings are sometimes replaced with something each cook thinks is best, such as cabbage, spinach or a selection of mixed vegetables. This certainly evokes a competitive spirit in all cooks! I also like this with plain boiled rice and poppadums.

1 Make the batter for the dumplings in a large bowl. Mix together the chick-pea flour, salt and bicarbonate of soda, then stir in about 125 ml (4 fl oz) water to make a batter with a thick dropping consistency. It should fall off the tip of a spoon without lingering. Leave to rest for at least 15 minutes.
2 Meanwhile, make sour yogurt for the curry in another bowl. Stir the yogurt and vinegar or citric acid together until blended.
3 Sift together the chick-pea flour, salt, ground coriander, chilli powder, turmeric and ground asafoetida. Make a well in the centre and stir in enough of the sour yogurt to form a smooth paste. Gradually stir in remaining yogurt. Stir in 1.2 litres (2 pints) water.
4 Heat the oil in a large, heavy-based saucepan or wok, then add the coriander and fenugreek seeds, dried red chillies and curry leaves and stir-fry until slightly darkened. Stir in the flour mixture and bring to the boil, then lower the heat and simmer, uncovered, for 15 minutes until thickened.
5 To fry the dumplings, heat more oil in a heavy-based saucepan until it is hot enough that a small amount of batter will immediately return to surface when it is dropped in. Drop in spoonfuls of batter without over-crowding the pan. Lower the heat and fry the dumplings until they are golden brown. Use a slotted spoon to remove the dumplings from the hot oil and drain on kitchen paper. Immediately transfer to curry mixture. Turn the heat back up to high and continue frying dumplings until all the batter has been used.
6 Transfer the curry and dumplings to a serving bowl and garnish with chopped coriander. Serve immediately.

SPICY POTATOES

Sookhe Aloo

Time to make: about 25 minutes
Time to cook: about 8 minutes
Serves 4 to 6

500 g (1 lb) potatoes

3 or 4 fresh green chillies

60 ml (2 fl oz) vegetable oil

2 teaspoons cumin seeds

large pinch ground asafoetida

1 tablespoon finely sliced peeled fresh root ginger

1 tablespoon salt

1 tablespoon ground coriander

2 teaspoons ground dried mango

½ teaspoon garam masala, see page 9

½ teaspoon chilli powder

½ teaspoon turmeric

2 tablespoons chopped fresh coriander leaves

sliced red chillies, optional, to garnish

Jeet Singh is my cook at home, and, as my daughter says, 'he makes these the best of anyone!' He has really mastered this dish, and this is his recipe. As well as serving this as a separate vegetable dish, it also makes a delicious filling for samosas and parathas, see page 27.

1   Put the potatoes in a large saucepan of water and bring to the boil, then continue boiling for 10 to 15 minutes until they are tender. Drain well and leave to cool.
2   Meanwhile, make a slit in each of the chillies.
3   When the potatoes are cool enough to handle, peel them. Break up the potatoes, one at a time, by holding them in your palm and closing your fist. Set aside.
4   Heat the oil in a heavy-based saucepan over a high heat, then add the cumin seeds and ground asafoetida.
5   When the seeds splutter, add the ginger and stir-fry until lightly fried. Add the potatoes and green chillies and continue stir-frying for about 1 minute until they look slightly glossy.
6   Add the salt, ground coriander, ground dried mango, garam masala, chilli powder, turmeric and 1 tablespoon of the chopped coriander, stirring to coat the potatoes in the spices.
7   Lower the heat and continue cooking, stirring occasionally, for about 5 minutes so the flavours blend. Transfer to a serving dish and garnish with remaining chopped coriander. Serve immediately.

RICE WITH PEAS

Mattar Ki Tahri

Time to make: 5 minutes, plus
  soaking
Time to cook: about 20 minutes
Serves 4 to 6

**315 g (10 oz) long-grain rice,
preferably basmati**

2 tablespoons vegetable oil

1 tablespoon cumin seeds

¼ teaspoon ground asafoetida

**1 kg (2 lb) fresh peas, shelled,
or 375 g (12 oz) frozen peas,
thawed**

2 tablespoons ground coriander

1 tablespoon salt

1 teaspoon chilli powder

**1 teaspoon garam masala, see
page 9**

1 teaspoon turmeric

I learned to make this not long after I was married. It was a favourite dish at my mother-in-law's home, so I felt it was a success when she asked for a second helping the first time I served it to her.

Here I give you the quantities to make this spiced pillau dish for a main course, so you can halve the quantities if you are serving it as an accompaniment, if you want. The spices are typical of northern Indian cooking, where this is often served simply with yogurt.

1 Put the rice in a fine sieve and rinse under running cold water until the water runs clear.
2 Put the rice and enough water to cover in a bowl and leave the rice to soak for 30 minutes. Drain the rice.
3 Heat the oil in a heavy-based saucepan or flameproof casserole over a high heat, then add the cumin seeds and the ground asafoetida.
4 When the seeds splutter, add the peas and rice, stirring to coat all the rice grains and peas in oil.
5 Stir in the ground coriander, salt, chilli powder, garam masala and turmeric and stir-fry until well blended together. Stir in 900 ml (32 fl oz) water and bring to the boil, uncovered.
6 When the water boils, cover the pan, lower the heat to low and simmer for about 10 minutes until all water is absorbed and grains are tender. Transfer to a serving dish and serve immediately.

CURRIED POTATOES

Aloo Dahiwala

Time to make: 5 minutes, plus
  boiling potatoes
Time to cook: about 25 minutes
Serves 4 to 6

---

500 g (1 lb) potatoes

3 or 4 fresh green chillies

2 tablespoons vegetable oil

1 teaspoon cumin seeds

large pinch ground asafoetida

**1 tablespoon finely chopped
peeled fresh root ginger**

125 g (4 oz) plain yogurt

2 teaspoons salt

2 teaspoons ground coriander

**½ teaspoon garam masala,
see page 9**

½ teaspoon turmeric

½ teaspoon chilli powder

**chopped fresh coriander leaves,
to garnish**

Here's a very potato popular preparation that goes particularly well with pooris, an unleavened fried bread. It is a speciality of the Uttar Pradesh region, where it is also made with very finely chopped raw unpeeled potatoes. In my opinion, the sourer tasting the yogurt, the better the dish.

1 Put the potatoes in a large saucepan of water and bring to the boil, then boil for 10 to 15 minutes until they are tender. Drain well and leave to cool.
2 Meanwhile, slit each of the green chillies.
3 When the potatoes are cool enough to handle, peel them. Break up potatoes, one at a time, by holding them in your palm and closing your fist so you end up with a lot of little pieces. Set the potatoes aside.
4 Heat the oil in a heavy-based saucepan over a high heat, then add the cumin seeds and ground asafoetida.
5 When the seeds splutter, add the ginger and stir-fry until slightly fried.
6 Lower the heat and beat in 1 tablespoon of the yogurt, beating until well blended. Continue beating in yogurt, 1 or 2 tablespoons at a time, until all the yogurt is incorporated.
7 Add the salt, ground coriander, garam masala, turmeric and chilli powder, stirring until well blended together. Stir in the broken up potatoes and green chillies, stir-frying for about 3 minutes until they look slightly fried.
8 Stir in 500 ml (16 fl oz) water and bring to the boil, then lower the heat and simmer, uncovered, for about 15 minutes until the gravy is thickened and the potatoes slightly crushed. Transfer to a serving dish and garnish with chopped coriander. Serve immediately.

*Menu 19: Spiced Rice, see page 59,
served with Curried Potatoes, above,
Sweet-and-Sour Pumpkin, see page 86,
and shop-bought poppadums.*

SWEET-AND-SOUR PUMPKIN

Khatta Mitha Kaddu

Time to make: 10 to 15 minutes
Time to cook: 35 to 40 minutes
Serves 4 to 6

---

750 g (1½ lb) pumpkin

4 or 5 fresh green chillies

60 ml (2 fl oz) vegetable oil

1 teaspoon fenugreek seeds

1 teaspoon cumin seeds

large pinch ground asafoetida

1 tablespoon sliced ginger

1 tablespoon sugar

1 tablespoon salt

1 tablespoon ground coriander

1 teaspoon garam masala

1 teaspoon chilli powder

½ teaspoon turmeric

22 g (¾ oz) tamarind pulp, diluted in 4 tablespoons water

chopped coriander, to garnish

The combination of tamarind and sugar in this dish makes it irresistible, even to those who do not generally eat pumpkin. This is especially good to serve with Wholemeal Parathas, see page 27, Chapatis, see page 62, or Pooris, fried unleavened bread, see below. Some people like to use the bread to mash the pumpkin to a soft mass, but I prefer to eat it chunky.

1   Peel the pumpkin, scoop out the fibres and seeds and cut into 4 cm (1½ in) cubes. Slit each of the green chillies.
2   Heat the oil in a heavy-based saucepan over a high heat, then add the fenugreek and cumin seeds and ground asafoetida.
3   When the seeds splutter, add the ginger and stir-fry for about 1 minute until lightly coloured. Stir in the pumpkin and chillies and continue stir-frying for 5 minutes until the pumpkin looks glossy. Stir in the sugar, salt, ground coriander, garam masala, chilli powder and turmeric, stirring until well blended together.
4   Cover the pan, lower the heat and simmer, stirring 2 or 3 times, for 20 to 30 minutes until the pumpkin is tender. Stir in tamarind juice and cook, stirring occasionally, for 2 to 3 minutes longer. Transfer to a serving dish and garnish with chopped coriander. Serve immediately.

POORIS

Because of the soft texture, this wholemeal bread is used for packed lunches. My recipe is for plain pooris, but you can also stuff them with cooked lentils, peas or potatoes. If your bread doesn't puff up while it fries, it probably means you need more practice rolling it out.

Rub 22 g (¾ oz) ghee the into 315 g (10 oz) plain wholemeal flour and ½ teaspoon salt in a bowl. Make a well in centre and add 125 ml (4 fl oz) water. Mix in flour from side of bowl and gradually add about 125 ml (4 fl oz) water, until a slightly sticky ball forms (you may not need all the water). Knead dough on lightly floured surface by folding it towards you and then pushing it away with the heel of your hand for about 3 minutes until it is soft and smooth. Your finger should need a bit of pressure to be pushed in. Shape dough into a ball and place back in bowl. Cover bowl with a damp cloth and leave the dough to rest

for at least 30 minutes.

Turn out dough on to a lightly floured surface and knead a little. Divide into 10 to 12 pieces and roll into smooth balls. Smear your hands with vegetable oil if dough sticks.

Roll out each ball on a greased surface until it is about 0.25 cm (⅛ in) thick. Rolling these out takes practice and you should not push rolling pin too firmly over dough. Turn flattened dough clockwise as you roll it, keeping it as round as possible. Roll it as thinly and evenly as possible without tearing. If the dough starts to stick, add a little extra oil to surface.

Heat vegetable oil in large frying pan until if a piece of dough is dropped in, it returns to surface immediately. Add poori and press with slotted spoon so it puffs up in centre. Use tongs to turn over and fry other side. Drain on kitchen paper and keep warm while frying remainder.

POTATOES WITH SESAME SEEDS

Til Aloo

Time to make: 5 minutes, plus
  cooking the potatoes
Time to cook: about 5 minutes
Serves 4 to 6

500 g (1 lb) potatoes

3 or 4 fresh green chillies

2 tablespoons sesame oil

30 g (1 oz) black sesame seeds

1 tablespoon salt

½ teaspoon turmeric

**2 tablespoons lime juice or
4 tablespoons lemon juice**

**chopped fresh mint or
coriander leaves, to garnish**

As children, my siblings and I looked forward to visiting our aunt, who always cooked this for us. The appearance was and still is quite intriguing. We used to love to eat these with plain yogurt and pooris – and I still do!

1   Put the potatoes in large pan of water and bring to the boil, then continue to boil for 10 to 15 minutes until they are tender. Drain well and leave to cool.

2   Meanwhile, chop each of the green chillies.

3   When the potatoes are cool enough to handle, peel them and cut them into 2.5 cm (1 in) cubes.

4   Heat the oil a heavy-based saucepan or wok over a high heat, then add the sesame seeds and stir-fry until they look glossy and fried. Add the green chillies and stir 2 or 3 times, then stir in the salt and turmeric, stirring until well blended together.

5   Add the potatoes and stir-fry until well coated with sesame seeds. Stir in lemon or lime juice. Transfer to a serving dish and garnish with chopped mint or coriander. Serve immediately.

SWEET-AND-SOUR YELLOW LENTILS

Khatti Meethi Dahl

Time to make: 10 minutes
Time to cook: 45 minutes to
 1 hour
Serves 4 to 6

185 g (6 oz) yellow lentils
1 tablespoon salt
1 tablespoon sugar
½ teaspoon turmeric
1 teaspoon garam masala, see page 9
1 teaspoon chilli powder
22 g (¾ oz) tamarind pulp, diluted in 4 tablespoons water, or 1 teaspoon concentrate
2 tablespoons vegetable oil or 30 g (1 oz) ghee, see page 18
1 teaspoon mustard seeds
7 to 8 fresh curry leaves or ½ teaspoon dried and crushed
chopped fresh coriander sprigs and lemon slices

For an authentic Maharashtrian flavour look for a masala mixture in Indian stores called *pav bhaji* masala. I particularly like to add this instead of the garam masala, although I have to admit most of my northern friends do not like it too strong. If I am eating on my own, I love to have this with just plain rice.

1 Rinse the lentils well, then drain them. Put the lentils in a large, heavy-based saucepan over a high heat. Add 1 litre (35 fl oz) water, the salt, sugar and turmeric.
2 Partially cover the pan and bring the water to the boil, then lower the heat and simmer, stirring occasionally, for about 45 minutes until the lentils are soft.
3 Stir in the garam masala, chilli powder and tamarind juice, stirring for 5 to 10 minutes until well blended together.
4 To temper the lentils, heat the oil or melt the ghee in another heavy-based saucepan or wok over a high heat, then add the mustard seeds and curry leaves. When the seeds splutter, stir in the lentil mixture and bring to the boil, then lower the heat and simmer for about 1 minute, stirring occasionally. Transfer to a serving dish and garnish with coriander and lemon slices. Serve immediately.

Menu 20: Potatoes with Sesame Seeds, see page 87, served with Sweet-and-Sour Yellow Lentils, above.

RICE PUDDING
Kheer

Time to make: 5 minutes
Time to cook: 40 to 45 minutes
Serves 4 to 6

1 litre (1¾ pints) whole milk
45 g (1½ oz) rice
125 g (4 oz) sugar
4 small green cardamom pods
2 or 3 leaves silver foil, optional
10 to 12 blanched almonds, slivered

Normally, I am not much of a dessert eater, but ever since I was a child I have never been able to resist this when it is served chilled. But, when it is served hot, I find it easy to pass on. This is a regular dessert in my home because both my husband and daughter also enjoy it.

The consistency of this pudding is a matter of individual taste, and you can use either long-grain or short-grain rice depending on what you have to hand. Unlike traditional Western rice puddings, this one isn't set but more like rice swimming in the milk, so once the rice is cooked in step 2 you can decide how thick you want it. Just keep cooking and stirring until you are happy. In southern India, *kheer* is called *payasam* and served much thinner than it is in the North.

Making this does involve a lot of stirring, but it is good served hot or cold, so you can easily make it a day ahead and keep it covered in the fridge until you are ready to serve.

1 Bring the milk to the boil over a medium heat in a heavy-based saucepan that has a capacity of double the amount of milk, stirring occasionally so it does not scorch.
2 When the milk boils, stir in the rice. Return the milk to the boil, then lower the heat to low and simmer, uncovered, for about 25 minutes until the rice is more than cooked and the milk is thickened. The colour may also be a bit darker.
3 When the milk mixture is as thick as you like, stir in the sugar and cardamom pods, stirring until the sugar dissolves and is blended. Continue cooking for 10 minutes. Transfer to a serving dish and garnish with silver foil, if desired, and slivered almonds. Serve immediately or refrigerate until ready to serve.

CARROT PUDDING
Gajar Ka Halwa

Time to make: 5 minutes
Time to cook: 34 to 40 minutes
Serves 4 to 6

---

1 kg (2 lb) carrots

1.2 litres (2 pints) whole milk

125 g (4 oz) sugar

30 g (1 oz) ghee, see page 18

1 teaspoon ground cardamom

12 flaked almonds

10 raisins, optional

Be sure to serve this piping hot because it becomes less tasty the cooler it gets. My husband thinks the perfect way to enjoy this is with a large dollop of clotted cream on top! I find this is a good dessert to have on hand if we have guests staying, because it keeps very well in the fridge for about two weeks, so I make it in double quantities and it is ready for re-heating whenever we want a dessert. It is also a good pudding to serve during the winter.

For a more authentic, brighter colour, use the red variety of carrots sold at Asian shops. Silver foil can be used for a more elaborate garnish, if you like. Add it before garnishing with the almonds and raisins.

1 Peel and grate the carrots.
2 Bring the milk and carrots to the boil in a large, heavy-based saucepan or wok. Continue cooking, stirring occasionally, for about 30 minutes until most of the milk has evaporated. You can cook over a high or a low heat, depending on how much time you have to stand and stir so the mixture does not scorch.
3 Stir in the sugar and continue stirring for about 5 minutes until it dissolves, most of the moisture has evaporated and the carrots have a slightly glossy look.
4 Stir in the ghee, ground cardamom and half the almonds and half the raisins, if desired. Transfer to a serving dish and garnish with remaining almonds and raisins. Serve immediately.

Cook's Tip
To save time, replace the whole milk with sweetened condensed milk and omit the sugar. It will take less time for the mixture to cook in step 2 and you can skip step 3.

INDIAN ICE CREAM
Kulfi

Time to make: about 45 minutes, plus cooling and freezing
Serves 8

1.2 litres (2 pints) whole milk
125 g (4 oz) sugar
4 or 5 green cardamom pods, seeds removed and crushed
12 to 15 blanched almonds
30 g (1 oz) shelled pistachio nuts
silver foil, to garnish, optional

This is a dessert few people make at home. I would never have thought about making it but about the time I bought a freezer, traditionally shaped *kulfi* moulds became readily available so I started experimenting. Now I realise how easy it is to have several batches with different flavours all made up. I find this is always appreciated because it is so unexpected.

1 Bring the milk to the boil in a heavy-based saucepan over a high heat. Lower the heat to medium and simmer the milk, uncovered, for 30 to 40 minutes until it is thickened and reduced to half the quantity, stirring occasionally so it does not scorch. The colour will change to a creamy beige and most of the bubbles will be in the centre. The wider the pan you use for this step, the quicker it will be.
2 Stir in the sugar, stirring until it dissolves. Bring the milk to the boil again, then lower the heat and simmer, uncovered, for 1 to 2 minutes, stirring occasionally. Stir in the cardamom seeds, then remove the pan from the heat and leave to cool.
3 Meanwhile, finely shred the blanched almonds and the pistachio nuts. When the thickened milk is cool, stir the almonds and pistachio nuts in, reserving a few of each for garnish.
4 Pour the mixture into 8 traditional *kulfi* moulds or individual freezerproof containers and freeze until solid. It should take 3 to 4 hours.
5 Remove the moulds or containers from the freezer and use a round-bladed knife to prise out the ice-cream into bowls. Garnish with silver foil, if desired, and the remaining almonds and pistachio nuts. Serve immediately.

Variations
You can use canned condensed milk along with the whole milk, to save time reducing the milk. In which case, you should also adjust the amount of sugar to taste.

This can also be flavoured with puréed fruit, the most popular being mango. Add the fruit at the start of step 3, stirring until it is well incorporated.

Top to bottom: Carrot Pudding, see page 91; Indian Ice Cream, above; Rice Pudding, see page 90.

SEMOLINA HALWA

Soojee Ka Halwa

Time to make: 2 minutes
Time to cook: about 20 minutes
Serves 4 to 6

90 g (3 oz) ghee, see page 18
125 g (4 oz) semolina
250 g (8 oz) sugar
¼ teaspoon ground cardamom
1 tablespoon flaked almonds, to garnish

A favourite of my daughter ever since she was a child! When she didn't want breakfast she would ask for this and because the semolina was good for her I didn't mind. In India, you will often find this served after Hindu religious ceremonies as *paarshad*.

1   Melt the ghee in a heavy-based saucepan over a high heat, then stir in the semolina. Stir-fry over a high heat at first and then over a lower heat so the semolina doesn't scorch for 4 to 5 minutes until the base of the pan looks glossy. At first the mixture will collect together in clumps but when it is ready it will not stick together too much.

2   At the same time, bring 900 ml (32 fl oz) water to the boil in another saucepan with a long handle. Add the sugar and stir to dissolve, then simmer, uncovered.

3   Add the sugar solution and the ground cardamom to the semolina and bring to the boil. Lower the heat and simmer, stirring occasionally, for 5 to 7 minutes until all the liquid is evaporated and there is a thin line of ghee around the edges. Transfer to a serving dish and garnish with the almonds. Serve immediately.

VERMICELLI PUDDING

Sevian Payasam

Time to make: 5 minutes
Time to cook: 30 to 40 minutes
Serves 4 to 6

1.2 litres (2 pints) whole milk
30 g (1 oz) cashew nuts or almonds
60 g (2 oz) vermicelli
30 g (1 oz) ghee, see page 18
2 green cardamom pods
10 to 12 raisins
125 g (4 oz) sugar

Like *kheer*, see page 90, this is a popular pudding in India but served with subtle differences throughout the country. When I was first served this in the South, I simply assumed the cook hadn't known how to make it properly because it was much thinner and with more liquid than I was used to. But my friend Nalini explained this was the preferred local style, and I began to appreciate how vastly different tastes are from one end of India to the other. This version is typical of the thicker northern preparation.

1 Bring the milk to the boil in a heavy-based saucepan over a high heat. Lower the heat and simmer the milk, uncovered, for 20 to 25 minutes until thickened and reduced to about half the quantity, stirring occasionally so it does not scorch. The colour will change to a creamy beige. The wider the pan you use for this step, the quicker it will be.

2 Meanwhile, cut each cashew nut or almond into 2 or 3 pieces and break the vermicelli into small pieces.

3 Melt the ghee in another heavy-based saucepan or wok over a medium heat. Add the nuts, cardamom pods and raisins and stir-fry until the nuts are light brown.

4 Use a slotted spoon to transfer the mixture to the thickened milk. Stir the vermicelli into the same ghee and stir-fry until lightly coloured. Add this and the sugar to the milk mixture, stirring until the sugar dissolves. Bring the milk to the boil again, then lower the heat and simmer, uncovered, for 5 minutes, stirring occasionally. Transfer to a serving dish and serve immediately, or cover and refrigerate until ready to serve.

INDEX